cook's library

Low Fat

cook's library

Low Fat

p

This is a Parragon Book
This edition published in 2003

Parragon
Queen Street House
4 Queen Street
Bath BA1 1HE, UK

ISBN: 0-75259-439-7

Printed in China

NOTE

This book uses metric and imperial measurements. Follow the same
units of measurement throughout; do not mix metric and imperial.
All spoon measurements are level: teaspoons are assumed to be 5 ml,
and tablespoons are assumed to be 15 ml. Unless otherwise stated,
milk is assumed to be full fat, eggs and individual vegetables, such as
potatoes, are medium, and pepper is freshly ground black pepper.

The times given for each recipe are an approximate guide only because
the preparation times may differ according to the techniques used by
different people and the cooking times may vary as a result of the type
of oven used. The preparation times include chilling and marinating
times, where appropriate.

Recipes using raw or very lightly cooked eggs should be
avoided by infants, the elderly, pregnant women, convalescents
and anyone suffering from an illness.

Contents

Introduction

Whether you follow a low-fat diet or simply want to introduce healthier eating habits to your lifestyle, this is the book for you. Although the majority of recipes are low in fat, some have been included because they are highly nutritious and add an important variety of ingredients.

Nutritionists agree that typical modern diets usually contain too much fat and that this can be detrimental to health. Yet, a moderate intake of fat is essential for good health. For example, the body requires fat-soluble vitamins. Fish oils are one of the richest sources of vitamins A and D, and vitamin E is found in vegetable oils. Fats are also a concentrated source of energy, providing over twice as much as carbohydrates or proteins. The aim should be to reduce fat in the diet, but not to cut it out altogether.

How much is too much?

The body's nutrient requirements, including the level of fat needed, vary with age, sex, general state of health, level of physical activity and even genetic inheritance. However, the proportions in which the different nutrients are required are much the same from one person to another. The World Health Organization recommends that fats should not exceed 30 per cent of the daily intake of energy. (Energy is measured in calories, kilocalories or kilojoules.) It has conducted studies in countries with an exceptionally high rate of heart disease and the research has revealed that this almost invariably coincides with a high-fat diet, where fats comprise as much as 40 per cent of the body's daily energy intake.

If 2,000 calories a day is taken as the average, then, for good health, only 600 of them should be supplied by fats. One gram of pure fat yields nine calories, whereas one gram of pure carbohydrate or pure protein yields only one calorie. Simple arithmetic, therefore, indicates that the maximum daily intake of fats, based on a daily intake of 2000 calories, should be 600 divided by nine, or 66.6 grams of fat.

Fats are broken down and digested in a different way from proteins and carbohydrates and the human body is designed to store them for times of need. However, in the Western world, food is no longer scarce and we do not need to rely on stored fat to provide the energy for day-to-day life. If a lot of fat is stored, the body becomes overweight, even obese. Worse still, a mechanism that is not yet fully understood can suddenly trigger fat deposits in the arteries, resulting in their becoming narrower and eventually leading to heart disease.

Types of Fat

Anyone who is already overweight and is keen to return to a healthier size can reduce their fat intake to well below the 30 per cent maximum. However, it is probably better and the long-term effects will be more permanent if the overall intake of calories is reduced, but the proportions of nutrients remains within the normal range. Everyone, overweight or not, should observe the no more than 30 per cent rule to ensure long-term health and vitality.

Fats are made up of a combination of fatty acids and glycerol. Fatty acids consist of a chain of carbon atoms linked to hydrogen atoms. The way these are linked determines the type of fat – saturated or unsaturated. The type of fat you eat is just as important as the amount.

Saturated fats

Saturated fatty acids contain as many hydrogen atoms as possible – there are no empty links on the chain. They are mainly found in animal products, such as meat and dairy foods, although some vegetable oils, including palm and coconut oil, also contain them. Foods containing hydrogenated vegetable oils, such as some types of margarine, also contain saturated fats as a by-product of their processing. They are easy to recognize as they are usually solid at room temperature.

These are the fats that the body has difficulty processing and which it tends to store. They also increase cholesterol levels in the bloodstream, which may increase the risk of heart disease. It is, therefore, sensible to reduce the level of saturated fats in the diet. They should comprise no more than 30 per cent of the total fat intake or no more than nine per cent of the total energy intake.

Unsaturated fats

These fatty acids have spare links in the carbon chain and some hydrogen atoms are missing. There are two types: monounsaturated fats which have one pair of hydrogen atoms missing and polyunsaturated fats which have more than one pair missing. These fats are normally liquid or soft at room temperature. They are both thought to contribute to reducing the level of cholesterol in the bloodstream.

Monounsaturated fats are mainly of vegetable origin, but are also found in oily fish, such as mackerel. Other rich sources include olive oil, many kinds of nuts, and avocados. There are two types of polyunsaturated fats: omega 3 is found in oily fish and omega 6 in seeds and seed oils, such as sunflower.

Cholesterol

The word cholesterol is almost certain to be heard in the course of virtually any discussion about diet and health, yet its role in the human body is far from fully understood. Although increased levels of dietary and blood cholesterol have been linked with heart disease, this is not the full story.

Cholesterol is a sterol that is found in all animal fats and in some plants. It is also synthesized by the human liver from cholesterol-free substances, so it quite clearly serves some useful purpose. It seems to be important in the production of some of the body's natural steroids and a derivative is converted to vitamin D by the action of sunlight on the skin.

To complicate matters further, there are two types of proteins that carry cholesterol in the bloodstream: low-density and high-density lipoproteins. It seems that low-density lipoproteins promote atherosclerosis, the condition in which fats (lipids) are deposited on the inner walls of the arteries, narrowing them and constricting the flow of blood. This, in turn, increases the risk of heart attacks and heart disease. High-density lipoproteins, on the other hand, appear to retard atherosclerosis.

Research continues, but it is apparent that cholesterol is not always a villain. Its effects – good or bad – are controlled by other factors. It is probably more sensible, therefore, to think in terms of overall reduction of fat intake, especially saturated fats, than worry about the cholesterol content of individual foods.

Cooking Techniques

Frying

This is undoubtedly the technique that most dramatically raises the level of fats in the diet. You do not have to abandon chips or sausages completely, but it is sensible to make sure that they are only occasional treats rather than a staple diet. Fried-food fans might find it helpful to know that ingredients absorb much more fat when shallow-fried than they do during deep-frying, but even deep-frying should be used only occasionally. If you do enjoy a shallow-fried dish once in a while, invest in a good quality, heavy-based, non-stick frying pan and you will require much less oil. Use a vegetable oil, high in polyunsaturates, for frying rather than a solid fat and measure the quantity you add to the pan. A spray oil is a useful way of controlling how much you use.

Try the Chinese cooking technique of stir-frying. The ingredients are cooked very rapidly over an extremely high heat, using a small amount of oil. Consequently, they absorb little fat and, as an additional advantage, largely retain their colour, flavour, texture and nutritional content.

Grilling

This is a good alternative to frying, resulting in foods with a similar crisp and golden coating, while remaining moist and tender inside. Ingredients with a delicate texture that can easily dry out, such as white fish or chicken breasts, will require brushing with oil, but more robust foods, such as red meat or oily fish, can usually be grilled without additional fat, providing the heat is not too fierce.

Consider marinating meat and fish in wine, soy sauce, cider, sherry, beer and herbs or spices. Not only will the marinade tenderize meat and provide additional flavour, it can be brushed on during grilling, so that additional fat is not required. When grilling, always place the food on a rack, so that the fat drains away.

Poaching

This is an ideal technique for ingredients with a delicate texture or subtle flavour, such as chicken and fish, and is fat free. Poached food does not have to be bland and uninteresting. You can use all kinds of liquids, including stock, wine and acidulated water, flavoured with vegetables and herbs. The cooking liquid can be used as the basis for a sauce to provide additional flavour, as well as preserving any nutrients.

Steaming

A fat-free technique, steaming is becoming an increasingly popular way of cooking meat, fish, chicken and vegetables. Ingredients retain their colour, flavour and texture, fewer nutrients leach out and it is a very economical method of cooking because steamers can be stacked on top of one another.

The addition of herbs and other flavourings to the cooking liquid or the ingredients being steamed, also results in a wonderfully aromatic dish.

An additional advantage of steaming is that when meat is cooked, the fat melts and drips into the cooking liquid below. In this case, do not use the cooking liquid for making , stocks, gravy or sauces.

Braising and stewing

Slow-cooking techniques produce succulent dishes that are especially welcome during the winter. Trim all visible fat from the meat and always remove the skin from chicken. If red meat is to be browned first, consider dry-frying it in a heavy-based pan and drain off any fat before continuing with the recipe. Straining the cooking liquid, reducing it and then skimming off the fat before serving is a classic way of preparing braised food and concentrates the flavour of the finished dish as well as reducing the fat content.

Roasting

Fat is an integral part of this cooking technique. Without it, meat or fish would dry out and become too brown. If you are planning a roast dish, stand meat on a rack over a tray or roasting tin so that the fat drains off. When making gravy, use stock or vegetable cooking water, rather than the meat juices.

Baking

Many baked dishes are virtually fat free. Foil- or baking paper- wrapped parcels of meat, fish or vegetables are always delicious, since they help to retain any juices and nutrients. Add a little fruit juice, cider, wine or sherry, rather than oil, butter or margarine, for a moist texture and delicious flavour.

Basic Recipes

These recipes form the basis of several of the dishes contained throughout this book. Many of these basic recipes can be made in advance and stored in the refrigerator until required.

Fresh Chicken Stock

MAKES
1.75 LITRES/3 PINTS

1 kg/2 lb 4 oz chicken, skinned
2 celery sticks , chopped
1 onion, sliced
2 carrots, chopped
1 garlic clove
few fresh parsley sprigs
2 litres/3½ pints water
salt and pepper

1 Place all the ingredients in a large saucepan and bring to the boil.

2 Skim away any surface scum using a large flat spoon. Reduce the heat to a gentle simmer, partially cover, and cook for 2 hours. Leave to cool.

3 Line a sieve with clean muslin and place over a large jug or bowl. Pour the stock through the sieve. The cooked chicken can be used in another recipe. Discard the other solids. Cover the stock and chill.

4 Skim away any surface fat before using. Store in the refrigerator for up to 3 days, or freeze in small batches until required.

Fresh Vegetable Stock

MAKES
1.75 LITRES/3 PINTS

1 large onion, sliced
1 large carrot, diced
1 celery stick , chopped
2 garlic cloves
1 dried bay leaf
few fresh parsley sprigs
pinch of grated nutmeg
2 litres/3½ pints water
salt and pepper

1 Place all the ingredients in a large saucepan and bring to the boil.

2 Skim away any surface scum using a large flat spoon. Reduce the heat to a gentle simmer, partially cover, and cook for 45 minutes. Leave to cool.

3 Line a sieve with clean muslin and place over a large jug or bowl. Pour the stock through the sieve. Discard the solids.

4 Cover the stock and store in the refrigerator for up to 3 days, until required, or freeze in small batches.

Fresh Fish Stock

MAKES
1.75 LITRES/3 PINTS

1 kg/2 lb 4 oz white fish bones, heads and scraps
1 large onion, chopped
2 carrots, chopped
2 celery sticks, chopped
½ tsp black peppercorns
½ tsp grated lemon rind
few fresh parsley sprigs
2 litres/3½ pints water
salt and pepper

1 Rinse the fish trimmings in cold water and place in a large saucepan with the other ingredients. Bring to the boil.

2 Skim away any surface scum using a large flat spoon.

3 Reduce the heat to a gentle simmer and cook, partially covered, for 30 minutes. Leave to cool.

4 Line a sieve with clean muslin and place over a large jug or bowl. Pour the stock through the sieve. Discard the solids. Cover the stock and store in the refrigerator for up to 3 days until required, or freeze in small batches.

Fresh Beef Stock

MAKES
1.75 LITRES/3 PINTS

about 1 kg/2 lb 4 oz bones from a cooked
 joint or raw chopped beef
2 onions, studded with 6 whole cloves, or
 sliced or coarsely chopped
2 carrots, sliced
1 leek, sliced
1–2 celery sticks, sliced
1 Bouquet Garni (see right)
about 2.25 litres/4 pints water

1 Use chopped marrow bones with
 a few strips of shin of beef, if
 possible. Put in a roasting tin and
 cook in a preheated oven,
 230°C/450°F/Gas Mark 8, for
 30–50 minutes, until browned.

2 Transfer to a large saucepan with
 the other ingredients. Bring to
 the boil and remove any scum
 from the surface with a large
 flat spoon.

3 Cover and simmer gently for
 3–4 hours. Strain the stock and
 leave to cool. Remove any fat
 from the surface and chill. If
 stored for more than 24 hours the
 stock must be boiled every day,
 cooled quickly and chilled again.

4 The stock may be frozen for up to
 2 months; place in a large plastic
 bag and seal, leaving at least
 2.5-cm/1-inch of headspace to
 allow for expansion.

Chinese Stock

MAKES
2.5 LITRES/4½ PINTS

750 g/1 lb 10 oz chicken pieces, trimmed
 and chopped
750 g/1 lb 10 oz pork spare ribs
3.75 litres/6 pints cold water
3–4 pieces of fresh root ginger, chopped
3–4 spring onions, each tied into a knot
3–4 tbsp Chinese rice wine or dry sherry

1 Place the chicken and pork in a
 large saucepan with the water.
 Add the ginger and spring onions.

2 Bring to the boil, and skim away
 any surface scum using a large
 flat spoon. Reduce the heat and
 simmer, uncovered, for at least
 2–3 hours.

3 Strain the stock, discarding the
 chicken, pork, ginger and spring
 onions. Add the Chinese rice wine
 and return to the boil, then
 reduce the heat and simmer for
 2–3 minutes. Leave to cool.

4 Refrigerate the stock when cool, it
 will keep for up to 4–5 days.
 Alternatively, it can be frozen in
 small batches and thawed
 as required.

Cornflour Paste

Mix 1 part cornflour with about
1.5 parts of cold water. Stir until
smooth. The paste can be used to
thicken sauces.

Fresh Bouquet Garni

1 fresh or dried bay leaf
few fresh parsley sprigs
few fresh thyme sprigs

Tie the herbs together with a length
of string or cotton.

Dried Bouquet Garni

1 dried bay leaf
good pinch of dried mixed herbs or any
one herb
good pinch of dried parsley
8–10 black peppercorns
2–4 cloves
1 garlic clove (optional)

Put all the ingredients in a small
square of muslin and secure with
string or cotton, leaving a long tail so
it can be tied to the handle of the
sauce pan for easy removal.

How to Use This Book

Each recipe contains a wealth of useful information, including a breakdown of nutritional quantities, preparation and cooking times, and level of difficulty. All of this information is explained in detail below.

A full-colour photograph of the finished dish.

The ingredients for each recipe are listed in the order that they are used.

The nutritional information provided for each recipe is per serving or per portion. Optional ingredients, variations or serving suggestions have not been included in the calculations.

The method is clearly explained with step-by-step instructions that are easy to follow.

Cook's tips provide useful information regarding ingredients or cooking techniques.

⭐ The number of stars represents the difficulty of each recipe, ranging from very easy (1 star) to challenging (4 stars).

🕐 This amount of time represents the preparation of ingredients, including cooling, chilling and soaking times.

🕐 This represents the cooking time.

Soups

The traditional way to start a meal is with a soup, but they can also be a satisfying meal in themselves depending on their ingredients and if they are served with crusty bread. For best results use home-made stock, made from the liquor left after cooking vegetables and the juices from fish and meat. Ready-made stocks in the form of cubes or granules tend to contain large amounts of salt and flavourings which can overpower delicate flavours. Although making fresh stock takes a little longer, it is well worth it for the superior taste. It is a good idea to make a large batch and freeze the remainder, in smaller quantities, for later use. Potato can be added to thicken soups rather than stirring in the traditional thickener of flour and water – or, worse, flour and fat.

This is a really hearty soup, filled with colour, flavour and goodness, which may be adapted to any vegetables that you have to hand.

Mixed Bean Soup

SERVES 4

1 tbsp vegetable oil
1 red onion, halved and sliced
100 g/3½ oz potato, diced
1 carrot, diced
1 leek, sliced
1 fresh green chilli, sliced
3 garlic cloves, crushed
1 tsp ground coriander
1 tsp chilli powder
1 litre/1¾ pints Fresh Vegetable Stock
   (see page 14)
450 g/1 lb mixed canned beans, such
   as red kidney, borlotti, black eye or
   flageolet, drained and rinsed
salt and pepper
2 tbsp chopped fresh coriander, to garnish

1 Heat the oil in a large, heavy-based saucepan and add the onion, potato, carrot and leek. Cook, stirring occasionally, for 2 minutes, until the vegetables have slightly softened.

2 Add the chilli and garlic and cook for a further minute.

3 Stir in the ground coriander, chilli powder and the vegetable stock.

4 Bring the soup to the boil, reduce the heat and cook for 20 minutes, or until the vegetables are tender.

5 Stir in the beans, season with salt and pepper to taste and cook, stirring occasionally, for a further 10 minutes.

6 Ladle the soup into bowls, garnish with chopped coriander and serve.

NUTRITION
Calories 190; Sugars 9 g; Protein 10g;
Carbohydrate 20 g; Fat 4 g; Saturates 0.5 g

 very easy

 5 mins

35 mins

 COOK'S TIP

Serve this soup with slices of warm corn bread or a cheese loaf.

This soup has a real Mediterranean flavour, using sweet red peppers, tomato, chilli and basil. It is great served with a warm olive bread.

Red Pepper Soup

1 Put the red peppers in a large, heavy-based saucepan with the onion, garlic and chilli. Add the passata and vegetable stock and bring to the boil over a medium heat, stirring constantly.

2 Reduce the heat and simmer for 20 minutes, or until the peppers have softened. Drain, reserving the liquid and vegetables separately.

3 Sieve the vegetables by pressing through a sieve with the back of a spoon. Alternatively, process in a food processor to a smooth purée.

4 Return the vegetable purée to a clean pan and add the reserved cooking liquid. Add the basil and heat through until hot. Garnish the soup with fresh basil sprigs and serve.

SERVES 4

225 g/8 oz red peppers, halved, deseeded and sliced
1 onion, sliced
2 garlic cloves, crushed
1 fresh green chilli, chopped
300 ml/10 fl oz passata
600 ml/1 pint Fresh Vegetable Stock (see page 14)
2 tbsp chopped fresh basil
fresh basil sprigs, to garnish

NUTRITION
Calories 55; Sugars 10 g; Protein 2 g; Carbohydrate 11 g; Fat 0.5 g; Saturates 0.1 g

 very easy

 5 mins

 25 mins

🍳 **COOK'S TIP**

This soup is also delicious served cold with 150 ml/5 fl oz natural yogurt swirled on the top just before serving.

Serve this soup over ice as a refreshing starter on a warm summer's day. It has the fresh tang of yogurt and a dash of spice from the Tabasco sauce.

Chilled Prawn *and* Cucumber Soup

SERVES 4

1 cucumber, peeled and diced
400 ml/14 fl oz Fresh Fish Stock
   (see page 14), chilled
150 ml/5 fl oz tomato juice
150 ml/5 fl oz low-fat natural yogurt
150 ml/5 fl oz low-fat fromage frais, or
   double the quantity of yogurt
125 g/4½ oz peeled, cooked prawns,
   thawed if frozen, chopped roughly
few drops of Tabasco sauce
1 tbsp chopped fresh mint
salt and white pepper
ice cubes, to serve

to garnish
fresh mint sprigs
cucumber slices
whole, peeled prawns

1 Place the cucumber in a blender or food processor and blend for a few seconds until smooth. (Alternatively, chop the cucumber finely and push through a sieve.)

2 Transfer the cucumber to a bowl. Stir in the stock, tomato juice, yogurt, fromage frais, if using, and prawns and mix well. Add the Tabasco sauce and season with salt and pepper to taste.

3 Stir in the chopped mint, cover and chill for at least 2 hours.

4 Ladle the soup into glass bowls and add a few ice cubes. Serve garnished with sprigs of fresh mint, cucumber slices and whole prawns.

NUTRITION
Calories *83*; Sugars *7 g*; Protein *12 g*;
Carbohydrate *7 g*; Fat *1 g*; Saturates *0.3 g*

 easy

2 hrs 15 mins

 0 mins

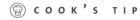 **COOK'S TIP**

Instead of prawns, add white crab meat or cooked minced chicken. For a vegetarian version, omit the prawns and add an extra 125 g/4½ oz cucumber, finely diced and use Fresh Vegetable Stock (see page 14) instead of Fish Stock.

Although this chilled soup is not an authentic Indian dish, it is wonderful served as a 'cooler' between hot, spicy courses.

Cucumber *and* Tomato Soup

1 Using a sharp knife, cut 1 tomato into 1-cm/½-inch dice.

2 Put the remaining tomatoes 3 into a blender or food processor and, with the motor running, add the cucumber, spring onions and watermelon. Blend until smooth.

3 If not using a food processor, push the deseeded watermelon through a sieve. Stir the diced tomatoes and mint into the melon mixture. Season with salt and pepper to taste. Finely chop the cucumber, spring onions and the remaining 3 tomatoes and add to the melon.

4 Chill the cucumber and tomato soup overnight in the refrigerator. Check the seasoning and transfer to a serving dish. Garnish with mint sprigs.

SERVES 4

4 tomatoes, peeled and deseeded

10-cm/4-inch piece cucumber, peeled, deseeded and chopped

2 spring onions, green part only, chopped

1.5 kg/3 lb 5 oz watermelon, peeled, deseeded and chopped

1 tbsp chopped fresh mint

salt and pepper

fresh mint sprigs, to garnish

NUTRITION

Calories *73*; Sugars *16 g*; Protein *2 g*; Carbohydrate *16 g*; Fat *1 g*; Saturates *0.2 g*

⭐⭐   easy

     2 hrs mins

     0 mins

(👨‍🍳) **COOK'S TIP**

Although this soup does improve if chilled overnight, it is also delicious as a quick appetizer if whipped up just before a meal, and served immediately.

This tasty red lentil soup, flavoured with chopped coriander, can easily be prepared in the microwave. The yogurt adds a light piquancy to the soup.

Red Lentil Soup *with* Yogurt

SERVES 4

2 tbsp butter
1 onion, chopped finely
1 celery stick, chopped finely
1 large carrot, grated
1 bay leaf
225 g/8 oz red lentils
1.25 litres/2 pints hot Fresh Vegetable or Chicken Stock (see page 14)
2 tbsp chopped fresh coriander
4 tbsp low-fat natural yogurt
salt and pepper
fresh coriander sprigs, to garnish

1 Place the butter, onion and celery in a large bowl. Cover and cook in a microwave on High power for 3 minutes.

2 Add the carrot, bay leaf and lentils. Pour in the stock. Cover and cook on High power for 15 minutes, stirring halfway through.

3 Remove the bowl from the microwave oven, cover and stand for 5 minutes.

4 Remove and discard the bay leaf, then process in batches in a food processor, until smooth. Alternatively, press the soup through a sieve.

5 Pour the soup into a clean bowl. Season with salt and pepper to taste and stir in the coriander. Cover and cook on High power for 4–5 minutes, until piping hot.

6 Serve in warm soup bowls. Place 1 tablespoon of the yogurt on top of each serving and garnish with sprigs of fresh coriander.

NUTRITION

Calories *280*; Sugars *6 g*; Protein *17 g*; Carbohydrate *40 g*; Fat *7 g*; Saturates *4 g*

easy

5 mins

30 mins

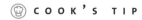 COOK'S TIP

For an extra creamy soup, try adding low-fat crème fraîche or soured cream instead of the yogurt.

This simple recipe includes sweet potato with its distinctive flavour and colour, combined with a hint of orange and fresh coriander.

Sweet Potato *and* Onion Soup

1 Heat the vegetable oil in a large, heavy-based saucepan and add the sweet potatoes, carrot, onions and garlic. Sauté the vegetables over a low heat, stirring constantly, for 5 minutes, until softened.

2 Pour in the vegetable stock and orange juice and bring to the boil.

3 Reduce the heat, cover and simmer for 20 minutes, or until the sweet potatoes and carrot are tender.

4 Transfer the mixture to a food processor or blender in batches and process for 1 minute, until puréed. Return the purée to the rinsed-out saucepan.

5 Stir in the yogurt and coriander and season with salt and pepper to taste.

6 Serve the soup in warm soup bowls and garnish with coriander sprigs and orange rind.

SERVES 4

2 tbsp vegetable oil
900 g/2 lb sweet potatoes, diced
1 carrot, diced
2 onions, sliced
2 garlic cloves, crushed
600 ml/1 pint Fresh Vegetable Stock (see page 14)
300 ml/10 fl oz unsweetened orange juice
225 ml/8 fl oz low-fat natural yogurt
2 tbsp chopped fresh coriander
salt and pepper

to garnish
fresh coriander sprigs
orange rind

NUTRITION

Calories *320*; Sugars *26 g*; Protein *7 g*; Carbohydrate *62 g*; Fat *7 g*; Saturates *1 g*

  very easy

  15 mins

  30 mins

🍳 COOK'S TIP

This soup can be chilled before serving, if preferred. If chilling, stir the yogurt into the dish just before serving. Serve in chilled bowls.

Packed full of flavour, this delicious fish dish is really a meal in itself, but it is ideal accompanied by a crisp side salad.

Fish *and* Crab Chowder

S E R V E S 4

1 large onion, chopped finely
2 celery sticks, chopped finely
150 ml/5 fl oz dry white wine
600 ml/1 pint fish stock
600 ml/1 pint skimmed milk
1 bay leaf
225 g/8 oz smoked cod fillet, skinned
    and cut into 2.5-cm/1-inch cubes
225 g/8 oz smoked haddock fillets, skinned
    and cut into 2.5-cm/1-inch cubes
2 x 175 g/6 oz canned crab meat, drained
225 g/8 oz French beans, sliced into 2.5-cm/
    1-inch pieces, blanched
225 g/8 oz cooked brown rice
4 tsp cornflour mixed with 4 tbsp water
salt and pepper
mixed green salad, to serve

1 Place the onion, celery and wine in a large, heavy-based saucepan. Bring to the boil, cover and cook over a low heat for 5 minutes.

2 Uncover the pan and cook for a further 5 minutes, until almost all of the liquid has evaporated.

3 Pour in the stock and milk and add the bay leaf, then bring to the boil. Reduce the heat, then stir in the cod and haddock. Simmer over a low heat, uncovered, for 5 minutes.

4 Add the crab meat, beans and cooked brown rice and simmer gently for 2–3 minutes, until just heated through. Remove the bay leaf with a slotted spoon and discard.

5 Stir in the cornflour mixture until the soup has thickened slightly. Season with salt and pepper to taste and ladle into warm soup bowls. Serve with a mixed green salad.

N U T R I T I O N
Calories *440*; Sugars *10 g*; Protein *49 g*;
Carbohydrate *43 g*; Fat *7 g*; Saturates *1 g*

easy

40 mins

30 mins

Carrot soup is very popular and here cumin, tomato, potato and celery add both richness and depth.

Carrot *and* Cumin Soup

1 Melt the butter in a large, heavy-based saucepan. Add the onion and garlic and cook very gently until softened.

2 Add the carrots and cook gently for a further 5 minutes, stirring frequently and taking care they do not brown.

3 Add the stock, cumin, celery, potato, tomato purée, lemon juice and bay leaves and season with salt and pepper to taste, then bring to the boil. Cover and simmer for about 30 minutes, until the vegetables are tender.

4 Remove and discard the bay leaves, cool the soup a little and then press it through a sieve or process in a food processor or blender until smooth.

5 Pour the soup into a clean pan, add the milk and bring to the boil over a low heat. Taste and adjust the seasoning, if necessary.

6 Ladle into warm soup bowls, garnish with a celery leaf and serve.

SERVES 4

3 tbsp butter or margarine
1 large onion, chopped
1–2 garlic cloves, crushed
350 g/12 oz carrots, sliced
900 ml/1½ pints Fresh Chicken or Vegetable Stock (see page 14)
¾ tsp ground cumin
2 celery sticks, sliced thinly
115 g/4 oz potato, diced
2 tsp tomato purée
2 tsp lemon juice
2 fresh or dried bay leaves
about 300 ml/10 fl oz skimmed milk
salt and pepper
celery leaves, to garnish

NUTRITION
Calories *114*; Sugars *8 g*; Protein *3 g*;
Fat *6 g*; Carbohydrate *12 g*; Saturates *4 g*

★★★ moderate

🕓 15 mins

🕐 45 mins

🍳 **COOK'S TIP**

This soup can be frozen for up to 3 months. Add the milk when reheating.

This nutritious soup uses split red lentils and carrots as its two main ingredients, and includes a selection of spices to give it a kick.

Spicy Dhal *and* Carrot Soup

SERVES 4

125 g/4½ oz split red lentils, rinsed
1.25 litres/2 pints Fresh Vegetable Stock
   (see page 14)
350 g/12 oz carrots, sliced
2 onions, chopped
225 g/8 oz can chopped tomatoes
2 garlic cloves, chopped
2 tbsp vegetable ghee or oil
1 tsp ground cumin
1 tsp ground coriander
1 fresh green chilli, deseeded and
   chopped, or 1 tsp minced chilli
½ tsp ground turmeric
1 tbsp lemon juice
salt
300 ml/10 fl oz milk
2 tbsp chopped fresh coriander
natural yogurt, to serve

1 Place the lentils in a large, heavy-based saucepan, together with 900 ml/ 1½ pints of the stock, the carrots, onions, tomatoes and garlic, then bring the mixture to the boil. Reduce the heat, cover and simmer for 30 minutes, or until the vegetables and lentils are tender.

2 Meanwhile, heat the ghee in a small pan. Add the ground cumin, ground coriander, chilli and turmeric and fry over a low heat for 1 minute. Remove from the heat and stir in the lemon juice. Season with salt to taste.

3 Process the soup in batches in a blender or food processor. Return the soup to the saucepan, add the spice mixture and the remaining stock and simmer over a low heat for 10 minutes.

4 Add the milk, taste and adjust the seasoning, if necessary. Stir in the fresh coriander and reheat gently. Serve in warm soup bowls with a swirl of yogurt on top.

NUTRITION
Calories *173*; Sugars *11 g*; Protein *9 g*;
Carbohydrate *24 g*; Fat *5 g*; Saturates *1 g*

very easy

15 mins

45 mins

A slightly hot and spicy Indian flavour is given to this soup with the use of garam masala, chilli, cumin and coriander.

Indian Potato *and* Pea Soup

1 Heat the vegetable oil in a large, heavy-based saucepan. Add the potatoes, onion and garlic and sauté over a low heat, stirring constantly, for about 5 minutes.

2 Add the garam masala, ground coriander and ground cumin and cook, stirring constantly, for 1 minute.

3 Stir in the vegetable stock and red chilli and bring the mixture to the boil. Reduce the heat, cover the pan and simmer for 20 minutes, until the potatoes begin to break down.

4 Add the peas and cook for a further 5 minutes. Stir in the yogurt and season with salt and pepper to taste.

5 Pour into warm soup bowls, garnish with fresh coriander and serve hot with warm bread.

SERVES 4

2 tbsp vegetable oil
225 g/8 oz floury potatoes, diced
1 large onion, chopped
2 garlic cloves, crushed
1 tsp garam masala
1 tsp ground coriander
1 tsp ground cumin
850 ml/1½ pints Fresh Vegetable Stock (see page 14)
1 fresh red chilli, chopped
100 g/3½ oz frozen peas
4 tbsp natural yogurt
salt and pepper
chopped coriander, to garnish
warm bread, to serve

NUTRITION
Calories *153*; Sugars *8 g*; Protein *6 g*; Carbohydrate *18 g*; Fat *6 g*; Saturates *1 g*

 very easy
15 mins
30 mins

 COOK'S TIP

For slightly less heat, deseed the chilli before adding it to the soup. Always wash your hands after handling chillies because they contain volatile oils that can irritate the skin and make your eyes burn if you touch your face.

This comforting broth is
perfect for a cold day and
is just as delicious made
with lean lamb or pork fillet.

Beef *and* Vegetable Soup

SERVES 4

55 g/2 oz pearl barley, soaked overnight
1.25 litres/2 pints Fresh Beef Stock
   (see page 15)
1 tsp dried mixed herbs
225 g/8 oz lean rump or sirloin beef,
   trimmed and cut into strips
1 large carrot, diced
1 leek, shredded
1 onion, chopped
2 celery sticks, sliced
salt and pepper
2 tbsp chopped fresh parsley, to garnish
crusty bread, to serve

1 Place the pearl barley in a large, heavy-based saucepan. Pour the stock over and add the mixed herbs, then bring to the boil. Reduce the heat, cover and simmer gently over a low heat for 10 minutes.

2 Skim away any scum that has risen to the top of the stock with a flat spoon.

3 Add the beef, carrot, leek, onion and celery to the pan. Bring back to the boil, cover and simmer for about 1 hour, or until the barley, meat and vegetables are just tender.

4 Skim away any remaining scum that has risen to the top of the soup with a flat ladle. Blot the surface with absorbent kitchen paper to remove any fat. Season with salt and pepper to taste.

5 Ladle the soup into warm soup bowls and sprinkle with fresh parsley. Serve piping hot, accompanied with crusty bread.

NUTRITION
Calories *138*; Sugars *2 g*; Protein *13 g*;
Carbohydrate *15 g*; Fat *3 g*; Saturates *1 g*

 moderate

 8 hrs 15 mins

1 hr 30 mins

🍳 **COOK'S TIP**

A vegetarian version can be made by omitting the beef and Fresh Beef Stock and using Fresh Vegetable Stock (see page 14) instead. Just before serving, stir in 175 g/6 oz fresh tofu, drained and diced.

A traditional clear soup made from beef bones and lean minced beef. Thin strips of vegetables provide a colourful garnish.

Consommé

1 Put the stock and minced beef in a large, heavy-based saucepan. Leave for 1 hour. Add the tomatoes, carrots, onion, celery, turnip, if using, bouquet garni, 2 of the egg whites, the crushed shells of 2 of the eggs and season with plenty of salt and pepper. Bring to almost boiling point, whisking continuously with a flat whisk.

2 Cover and simmer for 1 hour, taking care not to allow the layer of froth on top of the soup to break.

3 Pour the soup through a muslin-lined sieve or scalded fine cloth, keeping the froth back until the last, then pour the ingredients through the cloth again into a clean pan. The resulting liquid should be clear.

4 If the soup is not quite clear, return it to the pan with another egg white and the crushed shells of 2 more eggs. Repeat the whisking process as before and then boil for 10 minutes; strain again.

5 Add the sherry, if using, to the soup and reheat gently. Place the garnish in the warm soup bowls and carefully pour in the soup. Serve with Melba toast.

SERVES 4

1.25 litres/2¼ pints Fresh Beef Stock (see page 15)
225 g/8 oz minced extra lean beef
2 tomatoes, peeled, deseeded and chopped
2 large carrots, chopped
1 large onion, chopped
2 celery sticks, chopped
1 turnip, chopped (optional)
1 Fresh Bouquet Garni (see page 15)
2–3 egg whites
shells of 2–4 eggs, crushed
1–2 tbsp sherry (optional)
salt and pepper
Melba toast, to serve

to garnish
julienne strips of raw carrot, turnip, celery or celeriac or a one-egg omelette, cut into julienne strips

NUTRITION
Calories *109*; Sugars *6 g*; Protein *13 g*; Carbohydrate *7 g*; Fat *3 g*; Saturates *1 g*

 challenging

1 hr 30 mins

1 hr 15 mins

A mouthwatering, healthy, garlicky vegetable, bean and bacon soup. Serve it with granary or crusty wholemeal bread.

Bacon, Bean *and* Garlic Soup

SERVES 4

225 g/8 oz lean smoked back bacon slices
1 carrot, sliced thinly
1 celery stick, sliced thinly
1 onion, chopped
1 tbsp oil
3 garlic cloves, sliced
700 ml/1¼ pints hot Fresh Vegetable Stock (see page 14)
200 g/7 oz canned chopped tomatoes
1 tbsp chopped fresh thyme
400 g/14 oz canned cannellini beans, drained and rinsed
1 tbsp tomato purée
salt and pepper
grated Cheddar cheese, to garnish

1 Chop 2 slices of the bacon and place in a bowl. Cook in the microwave on High power for 3–4 minutes, until the fat runs out and the bacon is well cooked. Stir the bacon halfway through cooking to separate the pieces. Transfer to a plate lined with kitchen paper and leave to cool. When cool, the bacon pieces should be crisp and dry.

2 Place the carrot, celery, onion and oil in a large bowl. Cover and cook on High power for 4 minutes.

3 Chop the remaining bacon and add to the bowl with the garlic. Cover and cook on High power for 2 minutes.

4 Add the stock, chopped tomatoes, thyme, beans and tomato purée. Cover and cook on High power for 8 minutes, stirring halfway through. Season with salt and pepper to taste. Ladle into warm soup bowls and sprinkle with the crisp bacon and grated cheese.

NUTRITION
Calories *261*; Sugars *5 g*; Protein *32 g*;
Carbohydrate *25 g*; Fat *8 g*; Saturates *2 g*

⭐⭐ easy
🕐 5 mins
🕐 20 mins

 COOK'S TIP

For a more substantial soup add 55 g/2 oz small pasta shapes or short lengths of spaghetti with the stock and tomatoes. You will also need to add an extra 150 ml/5 fl oz vegetable stock.

You can use either yellow or green split peas in this recipe, but both types must be well rinsed and soaked overnight before use.

Split Pea *and* Ham Soup

1 Place the split peas in a bowl with half of the water and leave to soak overnight.

2 Put the soaked peas and their liquor, the remaining water, the onions, turnip, carrots and celery into a large, heavy-based saucepan, then add the ham knuckle, bouquet garni, dried thyme and ginger and bring to the boil.

3 Remove any scum from the surface of the soup. Reduce the heat, cover and simmer gently for 2–2½ hours, until the peas are very tender.

4 Remove the ham knuckle and bouquet garni. Remove about 125–175 g/ 4½–6 oz meat from the knuckle and finely chop it .

5 Add the chopped ham and vinegar to the soup and season with salt and pepper to taste.

6 Bring back to the boil, then reduce the heat and simmer for 3–4 minutes before serving.

SERVES 4

300 g/10½ oz dried yellow split peas, rinsed
1.75 litres/3 pints water
2 onions, chopped finely
1 small turnip, chopped finely
2 carrots, chopped finely
2–4 celery sticks, chopped finely
1 lean ham knuckle
1 Fresh Bouquet Garni (see page 15)
½ tsp dried thyme
½ tsp ground ginger
1 tbsp white wine vinegar
salt and pepper

NUTRITION
Calories *323*; Sugars *9 g*; Protein *17 g*;
Carbohydrate *45 g*; Fat *9 g*; Saturates *4 g*

⭐⭐   easy
     8 hrs 15 mins
     2 hrs 45 mins

 COOK'S TIP

If preferred, this soup can be sieved or blended in a food processor or blender until smooth. You can vary the vegetables, depending on what is available. Leeks, celeriac, or chopped tomatoes are particularly good.

This satisfying soup can be served as a main course. You can add rice and sweet peppers to make it even more hearty, as well as colourful.

Chicken *and* Leek Soup

SERVES 4

25 g/1 oz butter
350 g/12 oz skinless, boneless chicken, cut into 2.5-cm/1-inch pieces
350 g/12 oz leeks, cut into 2.5-cm/1-inch pieces
1.25 litres/2 pints Fresh Chicken Stock (see page 14)
1 Dried Bouquet Garni (see page 15)
8 stoned prunes, halved
salt and white pepper

1 Melt the butter in a large, heavy-based saucepan. Add the chicken and leeks to the saucepan and fry for 8 minutes.

2 Add the chicken stock and bouquet garni and stir well. Season with salt and pepper to taste.

3 Bring the soup to the boil, then reduce the heat and simmer for 45 minutes.

4 Add the prunes to the saucepan and simmer for about 20 minutes.

5 Remove the bouquet garni sachet from the soup and discard. Serve the soup in warm soup bowls.

NUTRITION
Calories *183*; Sugars *4 g*; Protein *21 g*;
Carbohydrate *4 g*; Fat *9 g*; Saturates *5 g*

 very easy

5 mins

1 hr 15 mins

🍳 **COOK'S TIP**

Instead of the Dried Bouquet Garni, you can use Fresh Bouquet Garni (see page 15) or a ready-made one. Choose herbs such as parsley, thyme and rosemary.

This fragrant, Thai-style soup combines citrus flavours with coconut and a hint of piquancy from the chillies.

Chicken *and* Coconut Soup

1 Place the coconut in a heatproof bowl and pour the boiling water over.

2 Place a fine sieve over another bowl and pour in the coconut water. Work the coconut through the sieve with a back of a spoon.

3 Add the coconut water, chicken stock, spring onions and lemon grass to a large, heavy-based saucepan.

4 Add the lime rind, juice, ginger, soy sauce and ground coriander to the saucepan.

5 Heat the pan to just below boiling point. Add the chicken and fresh coriander to the pan, then bring to the boil. Reduce the heat and simmer for 10 minutes.

6 Discard the lemon grass, lime rind and chillies. Pour the blended cornflour mixture into the saucepan and stir until slightly thickened. Season with salt and pepper to taste, then garnish with the chopped red chilli.

SERVES 4

125 g/4¹/₄ oz unsweetened
   desiccated coconut
500 ml/18 fl oz boiling water
500 ml/18 fl oz Fresh Chicken Stock
   (see page 14)
4 spring onions, sliced thinly
2 lemon grass stalks, outer leaves removed
sliced rind and juice of 1 lime
1 tsp grated fresh root ginger
1 tbsp light soy sauce
2 tsp ground coriander
2 large fresh red chillies, bruised
350 g/12 oz cooked, skinless, boneless
   chicken breast, cut into thin strips
1 tbsp chopped fresh coriander
1 tbsp cornflour mixed with
   2 tbsp cold water
salt and white pepper
chopped fresh red chilli, to garnish

NUTRITION
Calories *345*; Sugars *2 g*; Protein *28 g*;
Carbohydrate *5 g*; Fat *24 g*; Saturates *18 g*

    easy

    15 mins

    15 mins

Juicy chunks of fish and sumptuous shellfish are cooked in a flavoursome stock. Serve with toasted bread rubbed with garlic.

Mediterranean Fish Soup

SERVES 4

1 tbsp olive oil
1 large onion, chopped
2 garlic cloves, chopped finely
450 ml/15 fl oz Fresh Fish Stock (see page 14)
150 ml/5 fl oz dry white wine
1 bay leaf
1 each fresh thyme, rosemary and
    oregano sprig
450 g/1 lb firm white fish fillets, such as cod,
    monkfish or halibut, skinned and cut into
    2.5-cm/1-inch cubes
450 g/1 lb fresh mussels, prepared
400 g/14 oz canned chopped tomatoes
225 g/8 oz peeled, cooked prawns, thawed
    if frozen
salt and pepper
fresh thyme sprigs, to garnish

to serve
lemon wedges
4 slices toasted French bread, rubbed
    with a cut garlic clove

NUTRITION
Calories 316; Sugars 4 g; Protein 53 g;
Carbohydrate 5 g; Fat 7 g; Saturates 1 g

 moderate

30 mins

15 mins

1 Heat the olive oil in a large, heavy-based saucepan and gently fry the onion and garlic for 2–3 minutes, until just softened.

2 Pour in the stock and wine and bring to the boil.

3 Tie the bay leaf and herbs together with clean string and add to the saucepan with the fish and mussels. Stir well, cover and simmer for 5 minutes.

4 Stir in the tomatoes and prawns and continue to cook for a further 3–4 minutes, until piping hot and the fish is cooked through.

5 Discard the herbs and any mussels that have not opened. Season with salt and pepper to taste, then ladle into warm soup bowls.

6 Garnish with fresh thyme sprigs and serve with lemon wedges and toasted bread.

Thai red curry paste is quite fiery, but adds a superb flavour to this soup. It is available in jars or packets from most supermarkets.

Coconut *and* Crab Soup

1 Heat the oil in a preheated wok or large, heavy-based saucepan, swirling it around to coat. Add the red curry paste and red pepper and stir-fry over a medium heat for 1 minute.

2 Add the coconut milk, fish stock and fish sauce and bring to the boil.

3 Add the crab meat, crab claws, fresh coriander and spring onions.

4 Stir the mixture well and heat thoroughly for 2–3 minutes, or until the soup is warmed through.

5 Transfer to warm soup bowls and serve hot.

SERVES 4

1 tbsp groundnut oil
2 tbsp Thai red curry paste
1 red pepper, halved, deseeded and sliced
600 ml/1 pint coconut milk
600 ml/1 pint Fresh Fish Stock (see page 14)
2 tbsp Thai fish sauce
225 g/8 oz canned or fresh white crab meat
225 g/8 oz fresh or frozen crab claws
2 tbsp chopped fresh coriander
3 spring onions, sliced

 COOK'S TIP

Clean the wok after use by washing it with water, using a mild detergent if necessary, and a soft cloth or brush. Dry thoroughly then wipe the surface all over with a little oil to protect it.

NUTRITION
Calories *122*; Sugars *9 g*; Protein *11 g*;
Carbohydrate *11 g*; Fat *4 g*; Saturates *1 g*

     moderate

    15 mins

    20 mins

This traditional Scottish soup is thickened with a purée of rice and crab meat cooked in milk. Add soured cream, if liked, at the end of cooking.

Partan Bree

SERVES 4

1 medium-sized boiled crab
85 g/3 oz long-grain rice
600 ml/1 pint skimmed milk
600 ml/1 pint Fresh Fish Stock (see page 14)
1 tbsp anchovy essence
2 tsp lime or lemon juice
1 tbsp chopped fresh parsley or
　1 tsp chopped fresh thyme
3–4 tbsp soured cream (optional)
salt and pepper
snipped fresh chives, to garnish

1 Remove and reserve all the brown and white meat from the crab, then crack the claws and remove and chop the meat; reserve the claw meat.

2 Put the rice and milk into a saucepan and bring slowly to the boil. Cover and simmer gently for about 20 minutes.

3 Add the reserved white and brown crab meat, except the claw meat and season with salt and pepper to taste, then simmer for a further 5 minutes.

4 Leave to cool a little, then press through a sieve, or blend in a food processor or blender, until smooth.

5 Pour the soup into a clean saucepan and add the fish stock and the reserved claw meat. Bring slowly to the boil, then add the anchovy essence and lime juice and adjust the seasoning. Simmer for a further 2–3 minutes.

6 Stir in the fresh parsley and then swirl soured cream, if using, on top of each serving. Garnish with fresh chives.

NUTRITION

Calories *112*; Sugars *5 g*; Protein *7 g*;
Carbohydrate *18 g*; Fat *2 g*; Saturates *0.3 g*

 easy

30 mins

35 mins

 COOK'S TIP

If you are unable to buy a whole crab, use about 175 g/6 oz frozen crab meat and thaw thoroughly before use; or use 175 g/6 oz canned crab meat and just drain thoroughly.

Smoked haddock gives this soup a wonderfully rich flavour, while the mashed potatoes and fromage frais thicken and enrich the stock.

Smoked Haddock Soup

1 Put the fish, onion, garlic and water into a large, heavy-based saucepan, then bring to the boil. Reduce the heat, cover and simmer over a low heat for 15–20 minutes.

2 Remove the fish from the pan. Strip off the skin and remove any bones and reserve both. Flake the flesh finely with a fork.

3 Return the skin and bones to the cooking liquid and simmer for 10 minutes. Strain, discarding the skin and bones. Pour the cooking liquor into a clean saucepan.

4 Add the milk and flaked fish and season with salt and pepper to taste . Bring to the boil, then reduce the heat and simmer for about 3 minutes.

5 Gradually whisk in sufficient mashed potato to give a fairly thick soup, then stir in the butter, then add the lemon juice to taste.

6 Add the fromage frais and 3 tablespoons of the fresh parsley. Reheat gently and adjust the seasoning, if necessary. Sprinkle with the remaining parsley and serve immediately.

SERVES 4

225 g/8 oz smoked haddock fillet
1 onion, chopped finely
1 garlic clove, crushed
600 ml/1 pint water
600 ml/1 pint skimmed milk
225–350 g/8–12 oz hot mashed potatoes
2 tbsp butter
about 1 tbsp lemon juice
6 tbsp low-fat natural fromage frais
4 tbsp chopped fresh parsley
salt and pepper

NUTRITION
Calories *169*; Sugars *8 g*; Protein *16 g*;
Carbohydrate *16 g*; Fat *5 g*; Saturates *3 g*

easy

25 mins

40 mins

Starters *and* Snacks

If you prefer not to start your meal with soup, then this chapter contains a range of starters to whet the appetite. There are low-fat starters from around the world, such as Thai Potato Crab Cakes with chilli and soy sauce dipping sauce, or Sweet and Sour Drumsticks, which are barbecued to give them a glossy glaze and are very low in fat. There are also attractive starters to impress your guests at a dinner party, for example, Turkey and Vegetable Loaf and Spinach Cheese Moulds. There is also a selection of pâtés, including Parsley, Chicken and Ham and Smoked Fish and Potato, as well as snacks, including Spicy Chickpeas.

This is a quick one-pan dish, which is ideal for a quick snack. Packed with colour and flavour, you can add any other vegetables you have to hand.

Potato *and* Mushroom Hash

SERVES 4

675 g/1½ lb potatoes, cubed
1 tbsp olive oil
2 garlic cloves, crushed
1 green pepper, halved, deseeded and cubed
1 yellow pepper, halved, deseeded and cubed
3 tomatoes, diced
75 g/2¾ oz button mushrooms, halved
1 tbsp Worcestershire sauce
2 tbsp chopped fresh basil
salt and pepper
fresh basil sprigs, to garnish
warm crusty bread, to serve

1 Cook the potatoes in a saucepan of boiling salted water for 7–8 minutes, until tender. Drain well and reserve.

2 Heat the oil in a large, heavy-based frying pan and cook the potatoes for 8–10 minutes, stirring until browned.

3 Add the garlic and green and yellow peppers to the frying pan and cook for 2–3 minutes.

4 Stir in the tomatoes and mushrooms and cook, stirring, for 5–6 minutes.

5 Stir in the Worcestershire sauce and the chopped basil and season with salt and pepper to taste. Garnish with the fresh basil and serve with warm crusty bread.

NUTRITION
Calories 378; Sugars 14 g; Protein 18 g;
Carbohydrate 20 g; Fat 26 g; Saturates 7 g

 very easy

15 mins

 30 mins

 **COOK'S TIP**

Most brands of Worcestershire sauce contain anchovies. If cooking for vegetarians, make sure you choose a vegetarian variety.

This tasty dip is great for livening up simply cooked vegetables. You can vary the vegetables according to the season.

Vegetables *with* Tahini Dip

1 Line the base of a steamer with baking parchment and arrange the broccoli florets, cauliflower florets, asparagus and onion pieces on top.

2 Bring a large saucepan of water to the boil, and place the steamer on the top. Sprinkle the vegetables with lime juice for extra flavour and steam for 10 minutes, until they are just tender.

3 Meanwhile, make the dip. Heat the oil in a small, heavy-based saucepan, add the garlic, chilli powder and seasoning to taste and fry gently for 2–3 minutes, until the garlic has softened.

4 Remove the saucepan from the heat and stir in the tahini and fromage frais. Return the pan to the heat and cook gently for 1–2 minutes without boiling. Stir in the chopped chives.

5 Remove the vegetables from the steamer and arrange them on a warmed serving platter.

6 Sprinkle the vegetables with the sesame seeds and garnish with chopped chives. Serve with the hot tahini dip.

SERVES 4

225 g/8 oz small broccoli florets
225 g/8 oz small cauliflower florets
225 g/8 oz asparagus, sliced into
  5-cm/2-inch lengths
2 small red onions, quartered
1 tbsp lime juice
2 tsp toasted sesame seeds
1 tbsp chopped fresh chives, to garnish

tahini dip
1 tsp sunflower oil
2 garlic cloves, crushed
1/2–1 tsp chilli powder
2 tsp tahini
150 ml/5 fl oz low-fat fromage frais
2 tbsp chopped fresh chives
salt and pepper

NUTRITION
Calories *126*; Sugars *7 g*; Protein *11 g*;
Carbohydrate *8 g*; Fat *6 g*; Saturates *1 g*

⭐⭐   easy
          5 mins
          20 mins

These flavour-packed little moulds are a perfect starter or a tasty light lunch. Serve them with warm pitta bread.

Spinach Cheese Moulds

SERVES 4

100 g/3½ oz fresh spinach leaves, rinsed
300 g/10½ oz skimmed milk soft cheese
2 garlic cloves, crushed
fresh parsley, tarragon and chive sprigs,
    chopped finely
salt and pepper

to serve
mixed salad leaves and fresh herbs
warm pitta bread

NUTRITION
Calories *119*; Sugars *2 g*; Protein *6 g*;
Carbohydrate *2 g*; Fat *9 g*; Saturates *6 g*

easy

1 hr 15 mins

5 mins

1 Pack the spinach leaves into a saucepan while they are still wet, cover and cook over a medium heat for about 3–4 minutes, until wilted – they will cook in the steam from the wet leaves (do not overcook). Drain well and pat dry with kitchen paper.

2 Line the base of 4 small pudding basins or individual ramekin dishes with baking paper. Line the basins or ramekins with the spinach leaves so that the leaves overhang the edges.

3 Place the cheese in a bowl and add the garlic and herbs. Mix together thoroughly and season with salt and pepper to taste.

4 Spoon the cheese and herb mixture into the basins or ramekins and pull over the overlapping spinach to cover the cheese or lay extra leaves to cover the top. Place a greaseproof paper disc on top of each one and weigh down with a 100 g/3½ oz weight. Chill in the refrigerator for 1 hour.

5 Remove the weights and peel off the greaseproof paper. Loosen the moulds gently by running a small palette knife around the edge of each mould and turn them out on to individual serving plates. Serve the moulds immediately with a mixture of salad leaves and fresh herbs, and warm pitta bread.

This pâté is easy to prepare and may be stored in the refrigerator for up to two days. Serve with small crispbread, Melba toast or crudités.

Potato *and* Bean Pâté

1 Cook the potatoes in a saucepan of boiling water for 10 minutes, until tender. Drain well and mash.

2 Transfer the potato to a food processor or blender and add the beans, garlic, lime juice and the fresh coriander. Season with salt and pepper to taste and process for 1 minute to make a smooth purée. Alternatively, mix the beans with the potato, garlic, lime juice and coriander and mash well.

3 Turn the purée into a bowl and add the yogurt. Mix together thoroughly.

4 Spoon the pâté into a serving dish and garnish with the fresh coriander. Serve at once or cover with clingfilm and leave to chill before use.

SERVES 4

100 g/3½ oz floury potatoes, diced
225 g/8 oz mixed canned beans, such as borlotti, flageolet and kidney beans, drained and rinsed
1 garlic clove, crushed
2 tsp lime juice
1 tbsp chopped fresh coriander, to garnish
2 tbsp natural yogurt
salt and pepper
fresh coriander sprigs, to garnish

NUTRITION
Calories 84; Sugars 3 g; Protein 5.1 g; Carbohydrate 15.7 g; Fat 0.5 g; Saturates 0.1 g

⭐⭐ easy
🕐 5 mins
🕐 10 mins

 COOK'S TIP

To make Melba toast, toast sliced bread lightly on both sides under a preheated high grill and remove the crusts. Split the toasted bread horizontally with a sharp knife. Cut into triangles and toast the untoasted sides.

Although avocados do contain fat, it is unsaturated. If they are used in small quantities you can still enjoy their creamy texture.

Potato Skins *with* Guacamole

SERVES 4

4 x 225g/8 oz baking potatoes
2 tsp olive oil
coarse sea salt and pepper
chopped fresh chives, to garnish

guacamole dip
175 g/6 oz ripe avocado, peeled and stoned
1 tbsp lemon juice
2 ripe, firm tomatoes, chopped finely
1 tsp grated lemon rind
100 g/3½ oz low-fat soft cheese with herbs and garlic
4 spring onions, chopped finely
a few drops of Tabasco sauce
salt and pepper

1 Bake the potatoes in a preheated oven, at 200°C/400°F/Gas Mark 6, for 1¼ hours. Remove the potatoes from the oven and allow to cool for 30 minutes. Increase the oven temperature to 220°C/425°F/Gas Mark 7.

2 Halve the potatoes lengthways and scoop out 2 tablespoons of the flesh, then slice the potatoes in half again. Place on a baking tray and brush the insides lightly with oil. Sprinkle with salt and pepper to taste. Bake for a further 25 minutes, until the potatoes are golden and crisp.

3 To make the guacamole dip, mash the avocado with the lemon juice. Add the remaining ingredients and mix.

4 Drain the potato skins on kitchen paper and transfer to a warmed serving platter. Garnish with chives. Pile the avocado mixture into a serving bowl.

NUTRITION
Calories *399*; Sugars *4 g*; Protein *10 g*;
Carbohydrate *59 g*; Fat *15 g*; Saturates *4 g*

easy

45 mins

1 hr 40 mins

🍳 COOK'S TIP

Mash the leftover potato flesh with natural yogurt and seasoning, and serve as an accompaniment.

A great texture and flavour are achieved by mixing white and granary flours with minced onion, grated cheese and fresh herbs.

Cheese, Herb *and* Onion Rolls

1 Sift the white flour with the salt, mustard and pepper into a large mixing bowl. Mix in the granary flour, herbs, spring onions and most of the cheese.

2 Blend the fresh yeast with the warm water or, if using dried yeast, dissolve the sugar in the water, sprinkle the yeast on top and leave in a warm place for about 10 minutes, until frothy. Add the yeast mixture to the dry ingredients and mix to form a firm dough, adding more flour if necessary.

3 Knead until smooth and elastic. Cover with an oiled polythene bag and leave in a warm place to rise for 1 hour, or until doubled in size. Knock back and knead the dough until smooth. Divide into 10–12 pieces and shape into round or long rolls, coils or knots.

4 Alternatively, make 1 large plaited loaf. Divide the dough into 3 even-sized pieces and roll each into a long, thin sausage and join at one end. Beginning at the joined end, plait to the end and secure. Place on greased baking sheets, cover with an oiled sheet of polythene and leave to rise until doubled in size. Remove the polythene.

5 Sprinkle the rolls or loaf with the rest of the cheese. Bake in a preheated oven, at 200°C/400°F/Gas Mark 6, for 15–20 minutes, for the rolls, or 30–40 minutes, for the loaf.

SERVES 4

225 g/8 oz strong white flour
1½ tsp salt
1 tsp dried mustard powder
good pinch of pepper
225 g/8 oz granary or malted wheat flour
2 tbsp chopped fresh mixed herbs
2 tbsp chopped finely spring onions
125–175 g/4½–6 oz mature low-fat Cheddar cheese, grated
15 g/½ oz fresh yeast; or 1½ tsp dried yeast plus 1 tsp caster sugar; or 1 sachet easy-blend yeast plus 1 tbsp oil
300 ml/10 fl oz warm water

NUTRITION
Calories *529*; Sugars *2 g*; Protein *24 g*; Carbohydrate *98 g*; Fat *7 g*; Saturates *4 g*

 moderate

1 hr 30 mins

 20–40 mins

These tea-time classics have been given a healthy twist by using low-fat soft cheese and reduced-fat Cheddar.

Cheese *and* Chive Scones

SERVES 4

225 g/8 oz self-raising flour
1 tsp powdered mustard
½ tsp cayenne pepper
½ tsp salt
100 g/3½ oz low-fat soft cheese with added herbs
2 tbsp fresh snipped chives, plus extra to garnish
100 ml/3½ fl oz skimmed milk, plus extra for brushing
55 g/2 oz reduced-fat mature Cheddar cheese, grated
low-fat soft cheese, to serve

1 Sift the flour, mustard, cayenne pepper and salt into a large mixing bowl.

2 Add the soft cheese to the mixture and mix together until well incorporated. Stir in the snipped chives.

3 Make a well in the centre of the ingredients and gradually pour in the milk, stirring, until the mixture forms a soft dough.

4 Turn the dough out on to a floured surface and knead lightly. Roll out until 2-cm/¾-inch thick and use a 5-cm/2-inch plain pastry cutter to stamp out as many rounds as you can. Transfer the rounds to a baking sheet.

5 Re-knead the dough trimmings together and roll out again. Stamp out more rounds – you should be able to make 10 scones in total.

6 Brush the scones with milk and sprinkle with the grated cheese. Bake in a preheated oven, 200°C/ 400°F/Gas Mark 6, for 15–20 minutes, until risen and golden. Transfer to a wire rack to cool.

7 Serve the scones warm with low-fat soft cheese, garnished with chives.

NUTRITION
Calories 297; Sugars 3 g; Protein 13 g;
Carbohydrate 49 g; Fat 7 g; Saturates 4 g

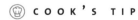
easy

10 mins

20 mins

 COOK'S TIP

For sweet scones, omit the mustard, cayenne pepper, chives and grated cheese. Replace the flavoured soft cheese with plain low-fat soft cheese. Add 75 g/ 2¾ oz currants and 25 g/1 oz caster sugar in step 2.

You can use dried chickpeas, soaked overnight, for this popular Indian snack, but the canned variety is just as flavoursome.

Spicy Chickpea Snack

1 Place the potatoes in a saucepan, add enough water to just cover and bring to the boil. Cover and simmer over a medium heat for 10 minutes, until tender. Drain and set aside.

2 Put the chickpeas into a bowl.

3 Combine the tamarind paste and water in a separate bowl. Add the chilli powder, sugar and 1 teaspoon salt and mix again. Pour the mixture over the chickpeas.

4 Add the onion and the potatoes to the chickpeas, and stir to mix taking care not to break up the potatoes. Season with pepper to taste.

5 Transfer to a serving bowl and garnish with tomatoes, if using, chillies and fresh coriander leaves.

SERVES 4

2 potatoes
400 g/14 oz canned chickpeas, drained
    and rinsed
2 tbsp tamarind paste
6 tbsp water
1 tsp chilli powder
2 tsp sugar
1 onion, chopped finely
salt and pepper

to garnish
1 tomato, sliced (optional)
2 fresh green chillies, chopped
fresh coriander leaves

NUTRITION
Calories *190*; Sugars *4 g*; Protein *9 g*;
Carbohydrate *34 g*; Fat *3 g*; Saturates *0.3 g*

⭐⭐   easy
     5 mins
     5 mins

🍳 **COOK'S TIP**

Chickpeas have a nutty flavour and slightly crunchy texture. Indian cooks also grind these to make a flour called gram flour, which is used to make breads, thicken sauces, and to make batters for deep-fried dishes.

Spanish onions are ideal for this recipe, as they have a mild, sweet flavour that is not too overpowering.

Baked Stuffed Onions

SERVES 4

4 large Spanish onions
2 slices streaky bacon, diced
½ red pepper, halved, deseeded and diced
125 g/4½ oz minced lean beef
1 tbsp chopped mixed fresh herbs, such as parsley, thyme and rosemary or 1 tsp dried mixed herbs
25 g/1 oz fresh white breadcrumbs
300 ml/10 fl oz Fresh Beef Stock (see page 15)
salt and pepper
long-grain rice, to serve
chopped fresh parsley, to garnish

gravy
25 g/1 oz butter
125 g/4½ oz mushrooms, chopped finely
300 ml/10 fl oz Fresh Beef Stock (see page 15)
2 tbsp cornflour
2 tbsp water

NUTRITION
Calories *182*; Sugars *6 g*; Protein *10 g*; Carbohydrate *18 g*; Fat *9 g*; Saturates *5 g*

 moderate
15 mins
2 hrs 15 mins

1 Put the onions in a saucepan of lightly salted water, then bring to the boil. Reduce the heat and simmer for 15 minutes, until tender.

2 Remove the onions from the saucepan, drain and cool slightly, then hollow out the centres and finely chop the inner flesh.

3 Heat a frying pan and cook the bacon until the fat runs out. Add the chopped onion and red pepper and cook for 5–7 minutes, stirring frequently.

4 Add the beef to the frying pan and cook, stirring, for 3 minutes, until browned. Remove from the heat and stir in the herbs, and breadcrumbs and season with salt and pepper to taste.

5 Grease an ovenproof dish and stand the whole onions in it. Pack the beef mixture into the centres and pour the stock around them.

6 Bake the stuffed onions in a preheated oven, 180°C/350°F/Gas Mark 4, for 1–1½ hours, or until tender.

7 To make the gravy, heat the butter in a small saucepan and fry the mushrooms for 3–4 minutes. Strain the liquid from the onions and add to the pan with the stock, then cook for 2–3 minutes.

8 Mix the cornflour with the water, then stir into the gravy and heat, stirring, until thickened and smooth. Season with salt and pepper to taste. Serve the onions with the gravy and rice, garnished with fresh parsley.

This delicious smoked fish pâté is given a tart, fruity flavour by the gooseberries, which complement the fish perfectly.

Smoked Fish *and* Potato Pâté

1 Cook the potatoes in a saucepan of boiling water for 10 minutes, until tender, then drain well.

2 Place the cooked potatoes in a food processor or blender.

3 Add the smoked mackerel and process for 30 seconds, until fairly smooth. Alternatively, place the ingredients in a bowl and mash with a fork.

4 Add the gooseberries, lemon juice and crème fraîche to the fish and potato mixture. Blend for a further 10 seconds or mash well.

5 Stir in the capers, gherkin, dill pickle and fresh dill. Season with salt and pepper to taste.

6 Spoon the fish pâté into a serving dish, garnish with lemon wedges and serve with slices of warm crusty bread.

SERVES 4

650 g/1 lb 7 oz floury potatoes, diced
300 g/10½ oz smoked mackerel, skinned and flaked
75 g/2¾ oz cooked gooseberries
2 tsp lemon juice
2 tbsp low-fat crème fraîche
1 tbsp capers
1 gherkin, chopped
1 tbsp chopped dill pickle
1 tbsp chopped fresh dill
salt and pepper
lemon wedges, to garnish
warm crusty bread, to serve

NUTRITION
Calories *418*; Sugars *4 g*; Protein *18 g*;
Carbohydrate *32 g*; Fat *25 g*; Saturates *6 g*

easy

20 mins

10 mins

  COOK'S TIP

Use stewed, canned or bottled cooked gooseberries for convenience and to save time, or when fresh gooseberries are out of season.

These small crab cakes are based on a traditional Thai recipe. They make a delicious snack when served with this sweet and sour cucumber sauce.

Thai Potato Crab Cakes

SERVES 4

450 g/1 lb floury potatoes, diced
175 g/6 oz white crab meat,
    drained if canned
4 spring onions, chopped
1 tsp light soy sauce
½ tsp sesame oil
1 tsp chopped lemon grass
1 tsp lime juice
3 tbsp plain flour
2 tbsp vegetable oil
salt and pepper

dipping sauce

4 tbsp chopped finely cucumber
2 tbsp clear honey
1 tbsp garlic wine vinegar
½ tsp light soy sauce
1 fresh red chilli, chopped

to garnish

1 fresh red chilli, sliced
cucumber slices

NUTRITION

Calories *254*; Sugars *9 g*; Protein *12 g*;
Carbohydrate *40 g*; Fat *6 g*; Saturates *1 g*

⭐⭐   easy

🕐   15 mins

🕐   25 mins

1 Cook the diced potatoes in a saucepan of boiling water for 10 minutes, until tender. Drain well and mash.

2 Mix the crab meat into the potato with the spring onions, soy sauce, sesame oil, lemon grass, lime juice and flour. Season with salt and pepper to taste.

3 Divide the crab and potato mixture into 8 equal portions and shape into small rounds, using floured hands.

4 Heat the oil in a heavy-based frying pan and cook the cakes, in batches of 4 at a time, for 5–7 minutes, turning once. Remove from the pan with a fish slice. Drain on kitchen paper and keep warm.

5 Meanwhile, make the dipping sauce. In a small serving bowl, mix together the cucumber, honey, vinegar, soy sauce and chilli.

6 Garnish the cakes with the red chilli and cucumber slices and serve with the dipping sauce.

🧑‍🍳 **COOK'S TIP**

When using lemon grass, remove the tough outer leaves and the root and finely chop.

Grilled mixed sweet peppers are filled with tender tuna, sweetcorn, nutty brown and wild rice and grated, reduced-fat Cheddar cheese.

Rice *and* Tuna Peppers

1 Place the wild rice and brown rice in separate saucepans, cover with boiling water and bring to the boil. Cook for about 40–50 minutes, or according to the instructions on the packet, until tender. Drain the rice well.

2 Meanwhile, preheat the grill to medium. Arrange the peppers on the grill rack, cut side down. Grill for 5 minutes, turn the peppers over and cook for a further 4–5 minutes.

3 Combine the cooked wild and brown rice to a large bowl and add the flaked tuna and drained sweetcorn. Gently fold in the grated cheese. Stir the basil leaves into the rice mixture and season with salt and pepper to taste.

4 Divide the tuna and rice mixture into 8 equal portions. Pile each portion into each cooked pepper half. Mix together the breadcrumbs and Parmesan cheese and sprinkle over each pepper.

5 Return the peppers to the grill for 4–5 minutes, until hot and golden brown.

6 Serve the peppers immediately, garnished with fresh basil and accompanied with fresh, crisp salad leaves.

SERVES 4

55 g/2 oz wild rice
55 g/2 oz brown rice
4 assorted peppers, halved and deseeded
200 g/7 oz canned tuna fish in brine, drained and flaked
325 g/11½ oz canned sweetcorn kernels, drained
100 g/3½ oz reduced-fat mature Cheddar cheese, grated
1 bunch fresh basil leaves, shredded
2 tbsp dry white breadcrumbs
1 tbsp freshly grated Parmesan cheese
salt and pepper
fresh basil leaves, to garnish
crisp salad leaves, to serve

NUTRITION
Calories *332*; Sugars *13 g*; Protein *27 g*; Carbohydrate *42 g*; Fat *8 g*; Saturates *4 g*

✪✪✪   moderate

    10 mins

1 hr 5 mins

This impressive-looking turkey loaf is flavoured with herbs and a layer of juicy tomatoes, then covered with thinly sliced courgette ribbons.

Turkey *and* Vegetable Loaf

SERVES 4

1 onion, chopped finely
1 garlic clove, crushed
900 g/2 lb lean turkey mince
1 tbsp chopped fresh parsley
1 tbsp chopped fresh chives
1 tbsp chopped fresh tarragon
1 egg white, lightly beaten
2 courgettes, 1 medium, 1 large
2 tomatoes, sliced thinly
salt and pepper
tomato and herb sauce, to serve

NUTRITION
Calories *165*; Sugars *1 g*; Protein *36 g*;
Carbohydrate *1 g*; Fat *2 g*; Saturates *0.5 g*

 easy

🕐 10 mins

🕐 1 hr 20 mins

1 Preheat the oven to 190°C/375°F/Gas Mark 5 and line a non-stick loaf tin with baking parchment. Place the onion, garlic and turkey in a bowl, add the herbs and season with salt and pepper to taste. Mix together with your hands, then add the egg white to bind.

2 Press half of the turkey mixture into the base of the tin. Thinly slice the medium courgette and arrange with the tomatoes over the meat. Top with the rest of the turkey mixture and press down firmly.

3 Cover with a layer of kitchen foil and place in a roasting tin. Pour in enough boiling water to come halfway up the sides of the loaf tin. Bake in the oven for 1–1¼ hours, removing the foil for the last 20 minutes of cooking. Test the loaf is cooked by inserting a skewer into the centre – the juices should run clear. The loaf will also shrink away from the sides of the tin.

4 Meanwhile, using a vegetable peeler or hand-held metal cheese slicer, cut the courgette into thin slices. Bring a saucepan of water to the boil and blanch the courgette ribbons for 1–2 minutes, until just tender. Drain and keep warm.

5 Remove the turkey loaf from the tin and transfer to a warm platter. Drape the courgette ribbons over the turkey loaf and serve with a tomato and herb sauce.

This recipe is bound to be popular with children and is very easy to prepare for their supper or tea.

Cranberry Turkey Burgers

1 Combine the turkey, onion, sage, breadcrumbs and cranberry sauce and season with salt and pepper to taste, then bind with the egg white.

2 Press into 4 x 10-cm/4-inch rounds, about 2-cm/³/₄-inch thick. Chill the burgers for 30 minutes.

3 Line a grill rack with baking parchment, making sure the ends are secured underneath the rack to ensure they don't catch fire. Place the burgers on top and brush lightly with oil. Put under a preheated moderate grill and cook for 10 minutes. Turn the burgers over, brush again with oil, then cook for a further 12–15 minutes until cooked through.

4 Fill the burger buns with lettuce, tomato and a burger and top with cranberry sauce. Serve with hot chips and salad garnish.

SERVES 4

350 g/12 oz minced lean turkey
1 onion, chopped finely
1 tbsp chopped fresh sage
6 tbsp dry white breadcrumbs
4 tbsp cranberry sauce
1 egg white, beaten lightly
2 tsp sunflower oil
salt and pepper

to serve
4 toasted granary or wholemeal
   burger buns
½ lettuce, shredded
4 tomatoes, sliced
4 tsp cranberry sauce

NUTRITION
Calories 209; Sugars 15 g; Protein 22 g;
Carbohydrate 21 g; Fat 5 g; Saturates 1 g

 easy

45 mins

25 mins

 COOK'S TIP

You can mince your own meat by choosing lean cuts and processing them in a blender or food processor.

Pâté is easy to make at home, and this combination of lean chicken, ham and herbs is especially straightforward.

Parsley, Chicken *and* Ham Pâté

SERVES 4

225 g/8 oz cooked skinless, boneless lean chicken, diced
100 g/3½ oz lean ham, diced
small bunch of fresh parsley
1 tsp grated lime rind, plus extra to garnish
2 tbsp lime juice
1 garlic clove, peeled
125 ml/4 fl oz low-fat natural fromage frais
salt and pepper

to serve
lime wedges
crispbread or Melba toast
green salad

1 Place the chicken and ham in a blender or food processor.

2 Add the parsley, lime rind and juice, and garlic and process until finely minced. (Alternatively, finely chop the chicken, ham, parsley and garlic and place in a bowl. Gently stir in the lime rind and lime juice.)

3 Transfer the mixture to a bowl and stir in the fromage frais. Season with salt and pepper to taste, cover with clingfilm and chill in the refrigerator for about 30 minutes.

4 Spoon the pâté onto individual serving dishes and garnish with extra grated lime rind. Serve the pâté with lime wedges, crispbread and a fresh green salad.

NUTRITION

Calories *119*; Sugars *2 g*; Protein *20 g*; Carbohydrate *2 g*; Fat *3 g*; Saturates *1 g*

 very easy

45 mins

0 mins

 COOK'S TIP

This pâté can be made successfully with other kinds of minced, lean, cooked meat, such as turkey, beef and pork. Alternatively, replace the meat with peeled prawns and/or white crab meat, or with canned tuna in brine, drained.

Chicken drumsticks are marinated to impart a tangy, sweet-and-sour flavour and a shiny glaze before being cooked on a barbecue.

Sweet *and* Sour Drumsticks

1 Skin the chicken drumsticks if desired and slash 2–3 times with a sharp knife. Put the chicken drumsticks into a non-metallic shallow dish, arranging them in a single layer.

2 Combine the vinegar, tomato purée, soy sauce, honey, Worcestershire sauce and garlic in a bowl. Season with cayenne pepper and salt and pepper to taste . Pour the mixture over the chicken, turning to coat. Cover and set aside in the refrigerator to marinate for 1 hour.

3 Cook the drumsticks on a hot barbecue or under a preheated grill for about 20 minutes, brushing with the glaze several times during cooking until the chicken is golden and the juices run clear when the thickest part is pierced with a skewer.

4 Transfer the drumsticks to a warm serving dish and serve immediately with crisp salad leaves.

SERVES 4

8 chicken drumsticks
4 tbsp red wine vinegar
2 tbsp tomato purée
2 tbsp soy sauce
2 tbsp clear honey
1 tbsp Worcestershire sauce
1 garlic clove, crushed
pinch of cayenne pepper
salt and pepper
crisp salad leaves, to serve

NUTRITION
Calories *171*; Sugars *9 g*; Protein *23 g*;
Carbohydrate *10 g*; Fat *5 g*; Saturates *1 g*

 very easy

 1 hr 15 mins

 20 mins

🧑‍🍳 **COOK'S TIP**

For a tangy flavour, add the juice of 1 lime to the marinade. While the drumsticks are grilling, check regularly to ensure that they are not burning on the outside.

The chicken filling for these easy-to-prepare tortillas has a mellow spicy heat. A fresh salad makes a perfect accompaniment.

Spicy Chicken Tortillas

SERVES 4

2 tbsp oil
8 skinless, boneless chicken thighs, sliced
1 onion, chopped
2 garlic cloves, chopped
1 tsp cumin seeds, crushed roughly
2 large dried chillies, sliced
400 g/14 oz canned tomatoes
400 g/14 oz canned red kidney beans, drained and rinsed
150 ml/5 fl oz Fresh Chicken Stock (see page 14)
2 tsp sugar
salt and pepper

to serve

1 large ripe avocado, peeled and stoned
1 lime
8 soft tortillas
225 ml/8 fl oz thick natural yogurt

1 Heat the oil in a large, heavy-based frying pan, add the chicken and fry for 3 minutes.

2 Add the onion and fry for 5 minutes, stirring until browned.

3 Add the garlic, cumin and chillies, and cook for about 1 minute.

4 Add the tomatoes, kidney beans, stock and sugar and season with salt and pepper to taste, then bring to the boil, breaking up the tomatoes. Reduce the heat, cover and simmer for 15 minutes. Remove the lid and cook for 5 minutes, stirring occasionally, until the sauce has thickened.

5 Mash the avocado with a fork.

6 Cut half of the lime into 8 thin wedges and reserve. Squeeze the juice from the other half of lime over the mashed avocado and mix well.

7 Warm the tortillas, according to the packet instructions. Put 2 tortillas on each serving plate, fill with the chicken mixture and top with spoonfuls of avocado and yogurt. Garnish with the reserved lime wedges.

NUTRITION
Calories *650*; Sugars *15 g*; Protein *48 g*; Carbohydrate *47 g*; Fat *31 g*; Saturates *10 g*

  easy

  10 mins

  35 mins

🍲 **COOK'S TIP**

If serving these to children, or if you want an even milder flavour, either remove the seeds from the chillies before using, or omit the chillies altogether.

A tasty alternative to traditional hamburgers, these lamb burgers are flavoured with mint jelly and accompanied with a smooth minty dressing.

Minty Lamb Burgers

1 Place the lamb in a large bowl and mix in the onion, breadcrumbs and mint jelly. Season well, then mould the ingredients together with your hands to form a firm mixture.

2 Divide the mixture into 4 and shape each portion into a round, measuring 10-cm/4-inches in diameter. Place the rounds on a plate lined with baking parchment and leave to chill for 30 minutes.

3 Preheat the grill to medium. Line a grill rack with baking parchment, securing the ends under the rack, and place the burgers on top. Grill for 8 minutes, then turn the burgers and cook the other side for a further 7 minutes, or until cooked through.

4 Meanwhile, make the relish. In a small bowl, mix together the fromage frais, mint jelly, cucumber and freshly chopped mint. Cover the relish with clingfilm and leave to chill in the refrigerator for 1 hour, or until required.

5 Drain the burgers on kitchen paper. Serve the burgers inside the baps with sliced tomatoes, cucumber, lettuce and relish.

SERVES 4

350 g/12 oz lean minced lamb,
1 onion, chopped finely
4 tbsp dry wholemeal breadcrumbs
2 tbsp mint jelly
salt and pepper

to serve

4 wholemeal baps, split
2 large tomatoes, sliced
small piece of cucumber, sliced
lettuce leaves

relish

4 tbsp low-fat natural fromage frais
1 tbsp mint jelly, softened
5-cm/2-inch piece of cucumber, diced finely
1 tbsp chopped fresh mint

NUTRITION
Calories *320*; Sugars *11 g*; Protein *28 g*;
Carbohydrate *33 g*; Fat *10 g*; Saturates *4 g*

 moderate

1 hr

 15 mins

These little meatballs, served with a minty yogurt dressing, can be prepared well in advance, ready to cook when required.

Lamb *and* Tomato Koftas

SERVES 4

225 g/8 oz finely minced lean lamb
1½ onions
1–2 garlic cloves, crushed
1 dried red chilli, chopped finely (optional)
2–3 tsp garam masala
2 tbsp chopped fresh mint
2 tsp lemon juice
salt
2 tbsp vegetable oil
4 small tomatoes, quartered
fresh mint sprigs, to garnish

yogurt dressing
150 ml/5 fl oz low-fat yogurt
5-cm/2-inch piece of cucumber, grated
2 tbsp chopped fresh mint
½ tsp toasted cumin seeds (optional)

1 Place the lamb in a bowl. Finely chop 1 onion and add to the bowl with the garlic and chilli, if using. Stir in the garam masala, mint and lemon juice and season well with salt. Mix well.

2 Divide the mixture in half, then divide each half into 10 equal portions and form each into a small ball. Roll the balls in the oil to coat. Quarter the remaining onion half and separate into layers.

3 Thread 5 of the spicy meatballs, alternating with the 4 tomato quarters and some of the remaining onion layers, on to each of 4 pre-soaked wooden or metal skewers.

4 Brush the vegetables with the remaining oil and cook the koftas under a preheated hot grill for about 10 minutes, turning frequently, until they are browned all over and cooked through.

5 Meanwhile, prepare the yogurt dressing for the koftas. In a small bowl mix together the yogurt, cucumber, mint and cumin seeds, if using.

6 Garnish the lamb and tomato koftas with mint sprigs and place on a large serving platter. Serve the koftas hot with the yogurt dressing.

NUTRITION
Calories *183*; Sugars *5 g*; Protein *15 g*;
Carbohydrate *5 g*; Fat *11 g*; Saturates *4 g*

easy

15 mins

10 mins

Lean ham wrapped around crisp celery, topped with a light crust of cheese and spring onions, makes a delicious light lunch.

Cheese *and* Ham Savoury

1 Lay the slices of ham on a chopping board. Place a piece of celery on each piece of ham and roll up. Place 3 ham and celery rolls in each of 4 small, heatproof dishes.

2 Sprinkle the spring onions over the ham and celery rolls and season with celery salt and pepper to taste.

3 Combine the soft cheese and yogurt and spoon the mixture over the ham and celery rolls.

4 Preheat the grill to medium. Sprinkle each portion with 1 tablespoon of the Parmesan cheese and grill for 6–7 minutes, until hot and the cheese has formed a crust. If the cheese starts to brown too quickly, lower the grill setting slightly.

5 Serve with a tomato and spring onion salad and crusty bread.

SERVES 4

12 thin slices of lean ham
4 celery sticks, each cut into 3 pieces, leaves reserved to garnish
1 bunch of spring onions, shredded finely
175 g/6 oz low-fat soft cheese with garlic and herbs
6 tbsp low-fat natural yogurt
4 tbsp freshly grated Parmesan cheese
celery salt and pepper

to serve
tomato salad
crusty bread

NUTRITION
Calories *140*; Sugars *3 g*; Protein *3 g*; Carbohydrate *20 g*; Fat *17 g*; Saturates *1 g*

 moderate

15 mins

10 mins

🍳 **COOK'S TIP**

Parmesan is a good cheese to use in low-fat recipes because its intense flavour means you need only a small amount.

Meat

The growing awareness of the importance of healthy eating means that supermarkets and butchers now offer leaner, lower-fat cuts of meat. Although these are slightly more expensive than standard cuts, you do not need to buy as much if you combine them with lots of tasty vegetables and low-fat sauces. It is also worth spending a little extra time cooking the meat carefully to enhance its flavour. Always remember to cut any visible fat from beef and pork before you cook it. Liver, kidney and venison are relatively low in fat. Look out for extra lean minced meats, which can be dry-fried without the addition of oil or fat.

Probably the best-known Mexican dish and a great favourite of many. The chilli content can be increased to suit your taste.

Chilli *con* Carne

SERVES 4

2 tbsp vegetable oil

750 g/1 lb 10 oz lean braising or stewing steak, cut into 2-cm/³/₄-inch cubes

1 large onion, sliced

2–4 garlic cloves, crushed

1 tbsp plain flour

425 ml/15 fl oz tomato juice

400 g/14 oz canned tomatoes

1–2 tbsp sweet chilli sauce

1 tsp ground cumin

425 g/15 oz canned red kidney beans, drained and rinsed

½ tsp dried oregano

1–2 tbsp chopped fresh parsley

salt and pepper

chopped fresh herbs, to garnish

to serve

plain rice

tortillas

1 Heat the oil in a large, flameproof casserole and fry the beef until well sealed. Remove the beef from the casserole.

2 Add the onion and garlic to the casserole and cook until lightly browned. Stir in the flour and cook for 1–2 minutes. Stir in the tomato juice and tomatoes and bring to the boil.

3 Return the beef to the casserole with the chilli sauce, ground cumin and season with salt and pepper to taste. Cover and cook in a preheated oven, 160°C/325°F/Gas Mark 3, for 1½ hours, until the beef is almost tender.

4 Stir in the beans, oregano and parsley and adjust the seasoning to taste. Cover the casserole and return to the oven for 45 minutes. Sprinkle with herbs and serve with plain rice and tortillas.

NUTRITION

Calories *443*; Sugars *11 g*; Protein *48 g*; Carbohydrate *30 g*; Fat *15 g*; Saturates *4 g*

easy

10 mins

2 hrs 45 mins

🍳 COOK'S TIP

Chilli con carne requires quite a lengthy cooking time, but you can save time and energy by preparing double the quantity you need and freezing half of it to serve on another occasion. Freeze for 3–4 weeks and thaw before use.

This is one of the best-known curries. Rogan Josh means 'red curry', and is so-called because of the red chillies in the recipe.

Rogan Josh

1 Heat the ghee in a large, flameproof casserole and brown the meat in batches. Remove the meat from the casserole and set aside in a bowl.

2 Add the onion to the ghee and cook over a high heat for 3–4 minutes, stirring occasionally.

3 In a bowl grind together the garlic, ginger, chillies, cardamom, cloves, coriander seeds, cumin seeds, paprika and salt. Add the spice paste and bay leaf to the casserole and stir until fragrant.

4 Return the meat and any juices in the bowl to the casserole and simmer for 2–3 minutes. Gradually stir the yogurt into the casserole, keeping the sauce simmering. Stir in the cinnamon stick and hot water, and pepper to taste.

5 Cover the casserole and cook in a preheated oven, 180°C/350°F/Gas Mark 4, for 1¼ hours, until the meat is very tender and the sauce is slightly reduced. Discard the cinnamon stick and stir in the garam masala. Remove any oil from the surface of the casserole before serving.

SERVES 4

2 tbsp ghee
1 kg/2 lb 4 oz lean braising steak, cut into 2.5-cm/1-inch cubes
1 onion, chopped finely
3 garlic cloves
2.5-cm/1-inch piece of fresh root ginger, grated
4 fresh red chillies, chopped
4 green cardamom pods
4 whole cloves
2 tsp coriander seeds
2 tsp cumin seeds
1 tsp paprika
1 tsp salt
1 bay leaf
125 ml/4 fl oz low-fat yogurt
2.5-cm/1-inch piece of cinnamon stick
150 ml/5 fl oz hot water
¼ tsp garam masala
pepper

NUTRITION

Calories 248; Sugars 2 g; Protein 35 g; Carbohydrate 2 g; Fat 11 g; Saturates 5 g

 moderate

10 mins

 1 hr 45 mins

Serve this old favourite with vegetables and herby dumplings for a substantial one-pot meal.

Boiled Beef *and* Carrots

SERVES 4

about 1.75 kg/3½ lb joint salted silverside or topside
2 onions, quartered, or 5–8 small onions
8–10 whole cloves
2 bay leaves
1 cinnamon stick
2 tbsp brown sugar
4 large carrots, sliced thickly
1 turnip, quartered
½ swede, sliced thickly
1 large leek, sliced thickly
25 g/1 oz butter or margarine
25 g/1 oz plain flour
½ tsp dried mustard powder
salt and pepper

dumplings

225 g/8 oz self-raising flour
½ tsp dried sage
90 g/3 oz shredded vegetable suet
about 150 ml/5 fl oz water

NUTRITION

Calories *459*; Sugars *2 g*; Protein *31 g*; Carbohydrate *35 g*; Fat *22 g*; Saturates *10 g*

 challenging

15 mins

2 hrs 45 mins

1 Put the beef in a large saucepan, add the onions, cloves, bay leaves, cinnamon and sugar and sufficient water to cover the meat. Bring slowly to the boil, removing any scum from the surface. Reduce the heat, cover and simmer gently for 1 hour.

2 Add the carrots, turnip, swede and leek, cover and simmer for a further 1¼ hours, until the beef is tender.

3 Meanwhile, make the dumplings. Sift the flour into a bowl, season well and mix in the herbs and suet. Add sufficient water to make a softish dough.

4 Divide the dough into 8 pieces, roughly shape into balls and place on top of the beef and vegetables. Replace the lid and simmer for 15–20 minutes.

5 Place the beef, vegetables and dumplings in a serving dish. Measure 300 ml/10 fl oz of the cooking liquid into a pan. Blend the margarine with the flour, then gradually whisk into the pan and bring to the boil. Reduce the heat and simmer until thickened. Stir in the mustard, adjust the seasoning and serve with the beef.

Minced lamb or beef is cooked here with onions, carrots, herbs and tomatoes and with a delicious topping of piped creamed potatoes.

Shepherd's Pie

1 Place the meat in a heavy-based saucepan with no extra fat and cook gently, stirring frequently, until the meat begins to brown.

2 Add the onions, carrots and garlic and continue to cook gently for about 10 minutes. Stir in the flour and cook for a minute or so, then gradually stir in the stock and tomatoes and bring to the boil.

3 Reduce the heat, add the Worcestershire sauce and herbs and season with salt and pepper to taste. Cover and simmer gently for about 25 minutes, stirring occasionally.

4 Cook the potatoes in boiling salted water until tender, then drain thoroughly and mash, beating in the butter, seasoning and sufficient milk to give a piping consistency. Place in a piping bag fitted with a large star nozzle.

5 Stir the mushrooms, if using, into the meat and adjust the seasoning. Turn into a shallow ovenproof dish.

6 Pipe the potatoes evenly over the meat. Cook in a preheated oven, 200°C/400°F/Gas Mark 6, for about 30 minutes, until piping hot and the potatoes are golden brown.

COOK'S TIP

If liked, a mixture of boiled potatoes and parsnips or swede may be used for the topping.

SERVES 4

700 g/1 lb 9 oz lean minced lamb or beef
2 onions, chopped
225 g/8 oz carrots, diced
1–2 garlic cloves, crushed
1 tbsp plain flour
200 ml/7 fl oz Fresh Beef Stock (see page 15)
200 g/7 oz canned chopped tomatoes
1 tsp Worcestershire sauce
1 tsp chopped fresh sage or oregano or
   ½ tsp dried sage or oregano
750 g–1 kg/1½–2 lb potatoes
25 g/1 oz butter or margarine
3–4 tbsp skimmed milk
125 g/4½ oz button mushrooms,
   sliced (optional)
salt and pepper

NUTRITION
Calories 378; Sugars 8g; Protein 33 g;
Carbohydrate 37 g; Fat 12 g; Saturates 4 g

★★★   moderate
    10 mins
        1 hr 30 mins

Fillet, sirloin, rump and entrecôte steaks are all suitable cuts for this dish, although rump retains the most flavour.

Steak *in a* Wine Marinade

SERVES 4

4 rump steaks, about 250 g/9 oz each
600 ml/1 pint red wine
1 onion, quartered
2 tbsp Dijon mustard
2 garlic cloves, crushed
4 large field mushrooms
salt and pepper
olive oil, for brushing
fresh rosemary branch (optional)

1 Snip through the fat strip on the steaks in 3 places, so that the steak retains its shape when barbecued.

2 Combine the red wine, onion, mustard and garlic and season with salt and pepper to taste. Lay the steaks in a non-metallic dish and pour the marinade over the meat. Cover and marinate in the refrigerator for 2–3 hours.

3 Remove the steaks from the refrigerator 30 minutes before you intend to cook them to let them come to room temperature. (This is especially important if the steak is thick, so that it cooks more evenly and is not well done on the outside and raw in the middle.)

4 Sear both sides of the steak – about 1 minute on each side – over a hot barbecue. If it is about 2.5-cm/1-inch thick, keep it over a hot barbecue and cook for a further 4 minutes on each side. This will give a medium-rare steak – cook it more or less, to suit your taste. If the steak is a thicker cut, move it to a cooler part of the barbecue or further away from the coals. To test if the meat is ready, simply press it with your finger – the more the meat yields, the less it is cooked.

5 Brush the mushrooms with the olive oil and cook them alongside the steak for 5 minutes, turning once. A the same time, put the rosemary branch, if using, in the fire to flavour the meat slightly.

6 Remove the steak and set aside to rest for 1–2 minutes before serving. Slice the mushrooms and serve immediately with the meat.

NUTRITION
Calories *356*; Sugars *2 g*; Protein *41 g*;
Carbohydrate *2 g*; Fat *9 g*; Saturates *4 g*

  easy

 2–3 hrs 10 mins

15 mins

This Japanese-style teriyaki sauce complements barbecued beef, but it can also be used to accompany chicken or salmon.

Beef Teriyaki

1 Place the meat in a shallow, non-metallic dish. To make the sauce, mix the cornflour with the sherry to make a smooth paste, then stir it into the vinegar, soy sauce, sugar, garlic, cinnamon and ginger. Pour the sauce over the meat, turn to coat and marinate in the refrigerator for at least 2 hours.

2 Remove the meat from the sauce, draining well. Pour the sauce into a small saucepan.

3 Cut the meat into thin strips and thread these, concertina-style, on to pre-soaked wooden skewers, alternating each strip of meat with pieces of spring onion and yellow pepper.

4 Gently heat the sauce until it is just simmering, stirring occasionally.

5 Barbecue the kebabs over hot coals for 5–8 minutes, turning and basting the beef and vegetables occasionally with the reserved teriyaki sauce.

6 Arrange the skewers on serving plates and pour the remaining sauce over the kebabs. Serve immediately with a green salad.

SERVES 4

450 g/1 lb extra thin lean beef steaks
8 spring onions, cut into short lengths
1 yellow pepper, deseeded and cut
   into chunks
green salad, to serve

sauce

1 tsp cornflour
2 tbsp dry sherry
2 tbsp white wine vinegar
3 tbsp soy sauce
1 tbsp dark muscovado sugar
1 garlic clove, crushed
½ tsp ground cinnamon
½ tsp ground ginger

NUTRITION
Calories *184*; Sugars *6 g*; Protein *24 g*;
Carbohydrate *8 g*; Fat *5 g*; Saturates *2 g*

   easy

  2 hrs 15 mins

15 mins

Serve these fruity, hot and spicy steaks with noodles. Use a non-stick ridged griddle pan to cook them to keep fat levels to a minimum.

Ginger Beef *with* Chilli

SERVES 4

4 lean beef steaks, such as rump, sirloin or fillet, about 100 g/3½ oz each, trimmed
2 tbsp ginger wine
2.5-cm/1-inch piece of fresh root ginger, chopped finely
1 garlic clove, crushed
1 tsp ground chilli
1 tsp vegetable oil
salt and pepper
fresh red chilli strips, to garnish

to serve
freshly cooked noodles
2 spring onions, shredded

relish
225 g/8 oz fresh pineapple, chopped
1 small red pepper, deseeded and chopped
1 fresh red chilli, deseeded and chopped
2 tbsp light soy sauce
1 piece of stem ginger in syrup, drained and chopped

NUTRITION
Calories *179*; Sugars *8 g*; Protein *21 g*;
Carbohydrate *8 g*; Fat *6 g*; Saturates *2 g*

 easy

 40 mins

10 mins

1 Using a meat mallet or covered rolling pin, pound the steaks until they are 1-cm/½-inch thick. Season on both sides with salt and pepper to taste and place in a shallow, non-metallic dish.

2 Combine the ginger wine, fresh root ginger, garlic and chilli and pour the mixture over the meat. Cover with clingfilm and chill for 30 minutes.

3 Place the pineapple in a bowl with the red pepper and chilli, then stir in the soy sauce and stem ginger. Cover with clingfilm and chill until required.

4 Brush a ridged griddle pan with the oil and heat until very hot. Drain the beef and add to the pan, pressing down to seal. Lower the heat and cook for 5 minutes. Turn the steaks over and cook for a further 5 minutes.

5 Drain the steaks on kitchen paper and transfer to warmed serving plates. Garnish with chilli strips and serve with noodles, spring onions and the fruit relish.

COOK'S TIP

You can cook the steak for more or less time according to how you like your meat, so cook it for longer if you like it well done.

Lean pork chops, stuffed with an aniseed and orange filling, are pan-cooked with fennel in a sweet sauce.

Pork *with* Fennel *and* Aniseed

1 Using a small, sharp knife, make a slit in the centre of each pork chop to create a pocket.

2 Mix the rice, orange rind, spring onions and aniseed together in a bowl. Season with salt and pepper to taste.

3 Spoon the rice mixture into the pocket of each chop, then press together gently to seal.

4 Heat the oil in a frying pan and fry the pork chops on each side for 2–3 minutes, until lightly browned.

5 Add the fennel and orange juice to the pan, then bring to the boil. Reduce the heat and simmer for 15–20 minutes, until the meat is tender and cooked through. Remove the pork and fennel with a slotted spoon and transfer to a serving plate.

6 Blend the cornflour and Pernod together in a small bowl. Add the cornflour mixture to the pan and stir it into the pan juices. Cook for 2–3 minutes, stirring, until the sauce has thickened.

7 Pour the Pernod sauce over the pork chops, garnish with fennel fronds and serve with broccoli florets.

SERVES 4

4 lean pork chops, about 125 g/4½ oz each, trimmed
55 g/2 oz brown rice, cooked
1 tsp orange rind, grated
4 spring onions, chopped finely
½ tsp aniseed
1 tbsp olive oil
1 fennel bulb, sliced thinly
450 ml/16 fl oz unsweetened orange juice
1 tbsp cornflour
2 tbsp Pernod
salt and pepper
fennel fronds, to garnish
broccoli florets, to serve

NUTRITION
Calories *298*; Sugars *10 g*; Protein *30 g*; Carbohydrate *18 g*; Fat *10 g*; Saturates *3 g*

✪✪✪ moderate

20 mins

30 mins

In this traditional Chinese dish the pork turns 'red' during cooking because it is basted in dark soy sauce.

Red Roast Pork *in* Soy Sauce

SERVES 4

450 g/1 lb lean pork fillet, trimmed
6 tbsp dark soy sauce
2 tbsp dry sherry
1 tsp Chinese five-spice powder
2 garlic cloves, crushed
2.5-cm/1-inch piece of fresh root ginger, chopped finely
1 large red pepper, halved, deseeded and cut into wedges
1 large yellow pepper, halved, deseeded and cut into wedges
1 large orange pepper, halved, deseeded and cut into wedges
4 tbsp caster sugar
2 tbsp red wine vinegar

to garnish
spring onions, shredded
snipped fresh chives

1 Place the pork in a shallow, non-metallic dish.

2 Mix together the soy sauce, sherry, Chinese five-spice powder, garlic and ginger. Spoon the mixture over the pork, cover and marinate in the refrigerator for at least 1 hour, or until required.

3 Remove the pork with a slotted spoon, reserving the marinade.

4 Put the pork on a roasting rack, placed over a roasting tin. Roast in a preheated oven, 190°C/375°F/Gas Mark 5, for 1 hour, occasionally basting with the marinade, until cooked through.

5 Meanwhile, arrange the red, yellow and orange peppers on a baking sheet and roast them with the pork for the last 30 minutes of the cooking time.

6 Place the caster sugar and vinegar in a saucepan and heat gently until the sugar dissolves, then bring to the boil. Reduce the heat and simmer for 3–4 minutes, until syrupy.

7 When the pork is cooked, remove from the oven and brush it with the sugar syrup. Leave for about 5 minutes, then slice and arrange on a serving platter with the peppers, garnished with spring onions and chives.

NUTRITION
Calories *268*; Sugars *20 g*; Protein *26 g*; Carbohydrate *22 g*; Fat *8 g*; Saturates *3 g*

  moderate

1 hr 15 mins

1 hr 15 mins

Tender, lean pork is cooked in a tasty, rich tomato sauce and flavoured with a tangy natural yogurt.

Pork Stroganoff

1 Heat the oil in a large, heavy-based saucepan and gently fry the pork, onion and garlic for 4–5 minutes, until they are lightly browned.

2 Add the flour and tomato purée, pour in the stock and stir until mixed thoroughly.

3 Add the mushrooms, green pepper and nutmeg. Season with salt and pepper to taste and bring to the boil. Reduce the heat, cover and simmer for 20 minutes, until the pork is tender and cooked through.

4 Remove the saucepan from the heat and stir in the yogurt.

5 Serve the pork and sauce on a bed of rice (sprinkled with chopped parsley) with an extra spoonful of yogurt, and garnish with a dusting of ground nutmeg.

SERVES 4

1 tbsp vegetable oil

350 g/12 oz lean pork fillet, cut into 1-cm/½ inch thick slices

1 onion, chopped

2 garlic cloves, crushed

25 g/1 oz plain flour

2 tbsp tomato purée

425 ml/15 fl oz Fresh Chicken or Vegetable Stock (see page 14)

125 g/4½ oz button mushrooms, sliced

1 large green pepper, halved, deseeded and diced

½ tsp ground nutmeg

4 tbsp low-fat natural yogurt, plus extra to serve

salt and pepper

plain rice, to serve

to garnish

chopped fresh parsley

ground nutmeg

NUTRITION

Calories *223*; Sugars *7 g*; Protein *22 g*; Carbohydrate *12 g*; Fat *10 g*; Saturates *3 g*

  easy

2 hrs 15 mins

30 mins

COOK'S TIP

You can buy ready-made fresh stock from leading supermarkets. Although more expensive, it is more nutritious than stock cubes, which are high in salt and artificial flavourings.

These pork and apple kebabs are served with a mustard sauce, making an ideal light lunch.

Pork *and* Apple Skewers

SERVES 4

2 eating apples, cored and cut into wedges
a little lemon juice
450 g/1 lb pork fillet, trimmed and cut into bite-sized pieces
1 lemon, sliced
2 tsp wholegrain mustard
2 tsp Dijon mustard
2 tbsp apple or orange juice
2 tbsp sunflower oil
crusty brown bread, to serve

mustard sauce
1 tbsp wholegrain mustard
1 tsp Dijon mustard
6 tbsp single cream

1 To make the mustard sauce, combine the wholegrain and Dijon mustards in a small bowl and slowly blend in the cream. Leave to stand until required.

2 Toss the apple wedges in the lemon juice to prevent any discoloration.

3 Thread the pork, apple and lemon slices alternately on to 4 metal or pre-soaked wooden skewers.

4 Mix together the wholegrain and Dijon mustards, apple juice and sunflower oil. Brush the mixture over the kebabs and barbecue over hot coals for 10–15 minutes, until cooked through, frequently turning and basting the kebabs with the mustard marinade.

5 Transfer the kebabs to warm serving plates and spoon a little of the mustard sauce over. Serve the kebabs with fresh, crusty brown bread.

NUTRITION
Calories *290*; Sugars *11 g*; Protein *24 g*;
Carbohydrate *11 g*; Fat *17 g*; Saturates *5 g*

easy

10 mins

15 mins

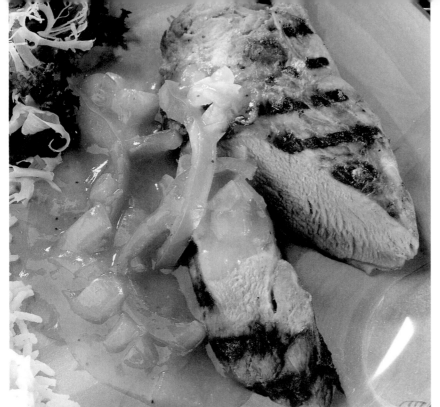

These tasty pork fillets are barbecued in a parcel of kitchen foil, then served with a tangy orange sauce.

Tangy Pork Fillet

1 Place a large piece of double thickness foil in a shallow dish. Put the pork fillet in the centre of the foil and season with salt and pepper to taste.

2 Heat the marmalade, orange rind and juice, vinegar and Tabasco sauce in a small saucepan, stirring until the marmalade melts and the ingredients combine. Pour the mixture over the pork and wrap the meat in foil, making sure that the parcel is well sealed so that the juices cannot run out. Place over hot coals and barbecue for about 25 minutes, turning occasionally.

3 For the sauce, heat the oil in a heavy-based saucepan and cook the onion for 2–3 minutes. Add the green pepper and cook for 3–4 minutes.

4 Remove the pork from the kitchen foil and place on the rack. Pour the juices from the meat into the pan with the sauce.

5 Barbecue the pork for a further 10–20 minutes, turning, until cooked through and golden on the outside.

6 In a small bowl, mix the cornflour with the orange juice to form a paste. Add to the sauce and cook, stirring, until the sauce has thickened. Slice the pork, spoon the sauce over and serve with rice and mixed salad leaves.

SERVES 4

400 g/14 oz lean pork fillet
3 tbsp orange marmalade
grated rind and juice of 1 orange
1 tbsp white wine vinegar
dash of Tabasco sauce
salt and pepper

sauce

1 tbsp olive oil
1 small onion, chopped
1 small green pepper, halved, deseeded and sliced thinly
1 tbsp cornflour
150 ml/5 fl oz orange juice

to serve

plain cooked rice
mixed salad leaves

NUTRITION
Calories *230*; Sugars *16 g*; Protein *19 g*;
Carbohydrate *20 g*; Fat *9 g*; Saturates *3 g*

⭐⭐ easy

🕐 10 mins

🕐 55 mins

In this dish, the lean and tender cuts of meat are perfectly complemented by the sweet apples and dry cider.

Pan-cooked Pork Medallions

SERVES 4

8 lean pork medallions, about 50 g/1¾ oz each
2 tsp vegetable oil
1 onion, finely sliced
1 tsp caster sugar
1 tsp dried sage
150 ml/5 fl oz dry cider
150 ml/5 fl oz Fresh Chicken or Vegetable Stock (see page 14)
1 green-skinned apple, cored and cut into 8 wedges
1 red-skinned apple, cored and cut into 8 wedges
1 tbsp lemon juice
salt and pepper
fresh sage leaves, to garnish

1 Discard the string from the pork and trim away any excess fat. Re-tie with clean string and set aside until required.

2 Heat the oil in a large, heavy-based frying pan and gently fry the onion for about 5 minutes, until softened. Add the sugar and cook for 3–4 minutes, until golden. Add the pork to the pan and cook for 2 minutes on each side until browned.

3 Add the sage, cider and stock, then bring to the boil. Reduce the heat and simmer for 20 minutes.

4 Meanwhile, toss the apple wedges in lemon juice so that they do not turn brown when exposed to the air.

5 Add the apples to the pork and mix gently. Season with salt and pepper to taste and cook for a further 3–4 minutes, until tender.

6 Remove the string from the pork and serve immediately, garnished with fresh sage leaves.

NUTRITION
Calories 256; Sugars 12 g; Protein 21 g; Carbohydrate 12 g; Fat 13 g; Saturates 3 g

 easy

20 mins

40 mins

 COOK'S TIP

Adding lemon juice to the cut apples pevents them from discolouring, making the end dish more attractive.

This is a pretty dish of pink tender lamb fillet served on a bed of light green mashed leeks and potatoes.

Lamb *with* Rosemary

1 Put the lamb in a shallow baking tin. Blend 2 tablespoons of the redcurrant jelly with the rosemary, garlic and seasoning. Brush the mixture over the lamb and cook in a preheated oven, 230°C/450°F/Gas Mark 8, brushing occasionally with any cooking juices, for 30 minutes.

2 Meanwhile, place the potatoes in a saucepan and cover with water. Bring to the boil, and cook for 8 minutes, until softened. Drain well.

3 Put the leeks in a saucepan with the stock, then bring to the boil. Reduce the heat, cover and simmer for 7–8 minutes, or until soft. Drain, reserving the cooking liquid.

4 Place the potato and leeks in a bowl and mash with a potato masher. Season with salt and pepper to taste and stir in the fromage frais. Transfer to a warm platter and keep warm.

5 In a saucepan, melt the remaining redcurrant jelly and stir in the leek cooking liquid. Boil for 5 minutes.

6 Slice the lamb and arrange it over the mash. Spoon the sauce over the top. Garnish the lamb with rosemary and redcurrants and serve with steamed carrots.

SERVES 4

500 g/1 lb 2 oz lean lamb fillet
4 tbsp redcurrant jelly
1 tbsp chopped fresh rosemary
1 garlic clove, crushed
450 g/1 lb potatoes, diced
450 g/1 lb leeks, sliced
150 ml/5 fl oz Fresh Vegetable Stock,
  (see page 14)
4 tsp low-fat natural fromage frais
salt and pepper
steamed carrots, to serve

to garnish
chopped fresh rosemary
redcurrants

NUTRITION
Calories *388*; Sugars *11 g*; Protein *35 g*;
Carbohydrate *38 g*; Fat *12 g*; Saturates *5 g*

✪✪✪   moderate

    15 mins

    55 mins

This classic recipe using lamb cutlets layered between sliced potatoes, kidneys, onions and herbs, makes a perfect meal on a cold winter's day.

Lamb Hotpot

SERVES 4

675 g/1 lb 8 oz waxy potatoes, sliced thinly
675 g/1 lb 8 oz lean lamb neck cutlets, trimmed
2 lamb's kidneys, sliced
1 large onion, sliced thinly
2 tbsp chopped fresh thyme
150 ml/5 fl oz lamb stock
25 g/1 oz butter, melted
salt and pepper
fresh thyme sprigs, to garnish

1 Arrange a layer of potatoes in the base of a 1.7 litre/3 pint ovenproof dish.

2 Arrange the lamb neck cutlets on top of the potatoes and cover with the kidneys, onion and chopped thyme.

3 Pour the lamb stock over the meat and season to taste with salt and pepper.

4 Layer the remaining potato slices on top, overlapping to completely cover the meat and onion.

5 Brush the potato slices with the melted butter, cover the dish and cook in a preheated oven, 180°C/350°F/Gas Mark 4, for 1½ hours.

6 Remove the lid and cook for a further 30 minutes, until the top is golden brown on top.

7 Garnish with the fresh thyme sprigs and serve hot.

NUTRITION
Calories 420; Sugars 2 g; Protein 41 g; Carbohydrate 31 g; Fat 15 g; Saturates 8 g

 easy
15 mins
2 hrs

 COOK'S TIP

Traditionally, oysters are also included in this tasty hotpot. Add them to the layers along with the kidneys, if wished.

Oranges and lamb are a great combination because the tangy citrus flavour offsets the fuller flavour of the meat.

Stir-fried Lamb *with* Orange

1 Heat a wok or large, heavy-based frying pan, without adding any oil.

2 Add the minced lamb to the wok. Dry-fry for 5 minutes, or until the lamb is evenly browned. Drain away any excess fat from the wok.

3 Add the garlic, cumin seeds, ground coriander and red onion to the wok and stir-fry for a further 5 minutes.

4 Stir in the orange zest and juice and the soy sauce, mixing until thoroughly combined. Cover, reduce the heat and simmer, stirring occasionally, for 15 minutes.

5 Remove the lid, increase the heat and add the orange segments. Stir to mix.

6 Season with salt and pepper to taste and heat through for a further 2–3 minutes.

7 Transfer the stir-fry to warm serving plates and garnish with snipped fresh chives. Serve immediately.

SERVES 4

450 g/1 lb minced lamb
2 garlic cloves , crushed
1 tsp cumin seeds
1 tsp ground coriander
1 red onion, sliced
finely grated zest and juice of 1 orange
2 tbsp soy sauce
1 orange, peeled and segmented
salt and pepper
snipped fresh chives, to garnish

NUTRITION
Calories 209; Sugars 4 g; Protein 25 g; Carbohydrate 5 g; Fat 10 g; Saturates 5 g

  easy

 5 mins

30 mins

🍲 **COOK'S TIP**
If you wish to serve wine with your meal, try light, dry white wines and lighter Burgundy-style red wines as they blend well with Oriental food.

These spicy lamb kebabs
go well with the cool
cucumber and yogurt dip.
In fine weather, the kebabs
can be barbecued.

Minty Lamb Kebabs

SERVES 4

2 tsp coriander seeds
2 tsp cumin seeds
3 whole cloves
3 green cardamom pods
6 black peppercorns
1-cm/½-inch piece of fresh root ginger
2 garlic cloves
2 tbsp chopped fresh mint
1 small onion, chopped
400 g/14 oz minced lamb
½ tsp salt
lime slices, to serve
fresh mint sprigs, to garnish

dip
150 ml/5 fl oz low-fat natural yogurt
2 tbsp chopped fresh mint
7-cm/3-inch piece of cucumber, grated
1 tsp mango chutney

1 Heat a frying pan and dry-fry the coriander seeds, cumin seeds, cloves, cardamom pods and peppercorns until they turn a shade darker and release a roasted aroma.

2 Grind the spices in a coffee grinder, spice mill or pestle and mortar.

3 Put the ginger and garlic into a food processor or blender and process to a purée. Add the ground spices, mint, onion, lamb and salt and process until finely chopped. (Alternatively, finely chop the garlic and ginger and mix with the ground spices and remaining kebab ingredients.)

4 Mould the kebab mixture into small sausage shapes on 4 metal or pre-soaked wooden skewers. Cook under a preheated hot grill for 10–15 minutes, turning the skewers occasionally.

5 To make the dip, mix together the yogurt, mint, cucumber and mango chutney in a small bowl.

6 Serve the kebabs with lime slices and the dip and garnish with fresh mint.

NUTRITION
Calories *295*; Sugars *4 g*; Protein *29 g*;
Carbohydrate *4 g*; Fat *18 g*; Saturates *9 g*

easy

5 mins

20 mins

👨‍🍳 COOK'S TIP

When dry-frying spices, watch them closely and move them around in the pan continuously, as they can turn bitter very quickly.

Minced lamb makes a very tasty and authentic moussaka. For a change, use minced beef instead.

Lamb *and* Potato Moussaka

1 Lay the aubergine slices on a clean surface or colander and sprinkle liberally with salt, to extract the bitter juices. Leave for 10 minutes, then turn the slices over and repeat. Rinse and drain well.

2 Meanwhile, heat the oil in a heavy-based saucepan and fry the onion and garlic for 3–4 minutes. Add the lamb and mushrooms and cook for 5 minutes, until browned. Stir in the tomatoes and stock, bring to the boil and simmer for 10 minutes. Mix the cornflour with the water and stir it into the pan, cook, stirring, until thickened.

3 Spoon half of the mixture into an ovenproof dish. Cover with the aubergine slices, then the remaining lamb mixture. Arrange the sliced potatoes on top.

4 Beat together the eggs, soft cheese and yogurt, and season with salt and pepper to taste. Pour the mixture over the potatoes to cover completely. Sprinkle with the Cheddar cheese.

5 Bake in a preheated oven, 190°C/375°F/Gas Mark 5, for 45 minutes, until the topping is set and golden brown. Garnish with flat-leaf parsley and serve with a green salad.

SERVES 4

1 large aubergine, sliced
1 tbsp olive or vegetable oil
1 onion, chopped finely
1 garlic clove, crushed
350 g/12 oz minced lean lamb
250 g/9 oz mushrooms, sliced
425 g/15 oz canned chopped tomatoes with herbs
150 ml/5 fl oz lamb or Fresh Vegetable Stock (see page 14)
2 tbsp cornflour
2 tbsp water
500 g/1 lb 2 oz potatoes, par-boiled for 10 minutes and sliced
2 eggs
125 g/4½ oz low-fat soft cheese
150 ml/5 fl oz low-fat natural yogurt
55 g/2 oz low-fat mature Cheddar cheese, grated
salt and pepper
fresh flat-leaf parsley, to garnish
green salad, to serve

NUTRITION
Calories *422*; Sugars *8 g*; Protein *32 g*; Carbohydrate *35 g*; Fat *18 g*; Saturates *8 g*

⭐⭐⭐⭐ challenging
🕐 30 mins
🕐 1 hr 5 mins

Dopiaza usually indicates a dish of meat cooked with plenty of onions; in this recipe the onions are cooked in two different ways.

Lamb Dopiaza

SERVES 4

2 tbsp ghee or vegetable oil
2 large onions, sliced finely
4 garlic cloves, 2 of them crushed
750 g/1 lb 10 oz lean boneless lamb, cut into 2.5-cm/1-inch cubes
1 tsp chilli powder
2.5-cm/1-inch piece fresh root ginger, grated
2 fresh green chillies, chopped
½ tsp ground turmeric
175 ml/6 fl oz low-fat natural yogurt
2 whole cloves
2.5-cm/1-inch cinnamon stick
300 ml/10 fl oz water
2 tbsp chopped fresh coriander
3 tbsp lemon juice
salt and pepper
naan bread, to serve

NUTRITION
Calories *433*; Sugars *6 g*; Protein *42 g*;
Carbohydrate *7 g*; Fat *27 g*; Saturates *8 g*

⭐⭐⭐   moderate

🕐   10 mins

🕐   1 hr 35 mins

1 Heat the ghee in a large, heavy-based saucepan and add 1 onion and all the garlic, then cook for 2–3 minutes, stirring constantly.

2 Add the lamb and cook until browned all over. Remove and set aside. Add the chilli powder, ginger, chillies and turmeric to the pan and stir for a further 30 seconds.

3 Add plenty of salt and pepper, the yogurt, cloves, cinnamon and water.

4 Return the lamb to the pan, then bring to the boil. Reduce the heat and simmer for 10 minutes.

5 Transfer the mixture to an ovenproof dish and cook uncovered in a preheated oven, 180°C/350°F/Gas Mark 4, for 40 minutes.

6 Adjust the seasoning, if necessary, stir in the remaining onion and cook uncovered for a further 40 minutes.

7 Add the fresh coriander and lemon juice.

8 Transfer the lamb to a warm serving dish and serve with naan bread.

Rich game is best served with a sweet fruit sauce. Here, the venison steaks are cooked with juicy prunes and redcurrant jelly.

Venison *and* Garlic Mash

1 Season the venison with salt and pepper on both sides. Heat the oil in a heavy-based frying pan and fry the venison with the onions for 2 minutes on each side until browned.

2 Reduce the heat and pour in the stock and wine. Add the redcurrant jelly and prunes and stir until the jelly melts. Cover and simmer for 10 minutes.

3 Meanwhile, make the garlic mash. Place the potatoes in a saucepan and cover with water. Bring to the boil and cook for 8–10 minutes, until tender. Drain well and mash until smooth. Add the garlic purée, fromage frais and parsley and blend thoroughly. Season, set aside and keep warm.

4 Remove the medallions from the frying pan with a slotted spoon and keep warm.

5 Blend the cornflour with the brandy in a small bowl and add to the pan juices. Heat, stirring, until thickened. Season with salt and pepper to taste. Serve the venison with the redcurrant and prune sauce, garlic mash and patty pans, if using.

SERVES 4

8 medallions of venison, about 75 g/2¾ oz each
1 tbsp vegetable oil
1 red onion, chopped
150 ml/5 fl oz Fresh Beef Stock (see page 15)
150 ml/5 fl oz red wine
3 tbsp redcurrant jelly
100 g/3½ oz ready-to-eat dried, pitted prunes
2 tsp cornflour
2 tbsp brandy
salt and pepper
patty pans, to serve (optional)

garlic mash
900 g/2 lb potatoes, diced
½ tsp garlic purée
2 tbsp low-fat natural fromage frais
4 tbsp chopped fresh parsley

NUTRITION
Calories *602*; Sugars *18 g*; Protein *51 g*; Carbohydrate *62 g*; Fat *14 g*; Saturates *1 g*

 moderate

10 mins

35 mins

 COOK'S TIP

If you cannot find garlic purée, simply cook peeled garlic cloves with the potatoes and mash with the potato mixture in step 3.

Poultry

Chicken and turkey contain less fat than red meats, and even less if you remove the skin first. Duck is a rich meat with a distinctive flavour, and you only need a small amount to create flavoursome dishes which are healthy too. As chicken does not have a very strong flavour, it marries well with other ingredients and the recipes in this chapter exploit that quality. Fruit features heavily in low-fat diets and it works particularly well with poultry. In this chapter there are several examples: Roast Duck with Apple, Pot-roast Orange Chicken and Lime Fricassée of Chicken. Grilling or barbecuing is a very healthy way to cook as it requires little or no fat, and it produces deliciously succulent meat with a crispy coating, for example, Mediterranean Chicken.

Make sure the barbecue or grill is really hot before you start cooking. The coals should be white and glow red when fanned.

Chicken *in* Spicy Yogurt

SERVES 4

3 dried red chillies
2 tbsp coriander seeds
2 tsp ground turmeric
2 tsp garam masala
4 garlic cloves, crushed
1/2 onion, chopped
2.5-cm/1-inch piece of fresh root
   ginger, grated
2 tbsp lime juice
1 tsp salt
125 ml/4 fl oz low-fat natural yogurt
1 tbsp oil
2 kg/4 lb 8 oz skinless chicken, cut into
   6 pieces, or 6 chicken portions
fresh mint sprigs, to garnish

to serve
tomatoes, chopped
cucumber, diced
red onion, sliced
raita

NUTRITION
Calories *74*; Sugars *2 g*; Protein *9 g*;
Carbohydrate *2 g*; Fat *4 g*; Saturates *1 g*

    moderate

4 hrs 45 mins

25 mins

1 Grind together the chillies, coriander seeds, ground turmeric, garam masala, garlic, onion, ginger, lime juice and salt in a pestle and mortar or grinder.

2 Gently heat a frying pan and add the spice mixture. Stir until fragrant, about 2 minutes, and turn into a shallow non-porous dish.

3 Add the natural yogurt and oil to the spice paste and mix well to combine.

4 Make 3 slashes in the flesh of each piece of chicken. Add the chicken to the dish containing the yogurt and spice mixture and coat the pieces completely in the marinade. Cover with clingfilm and chill for at least 4 hours. Remove the dish from the refrigerator and leave covered at room temperature for 30 minutes before cooking.

5 Wrap the chicken pieces in foil, sealing well so the juices cannot escape.

6 Cook the chicken pieces over a very hot barbecue for about 15 minutes, turning once.

7 Remove the foil, with tongs, and brown the chicken on the barbecue for a further 5 minutes.

8 Serve the chicken with the tomatoes, cucumber, red onion and the raita. Garnish with mint sprigs.

Traditionally, chicken tikka is cooked in a fiery-hot clay tandoori oven, but it works well on the barbecue, too.

Chicken Tikka

1 Place the chicken pieces in a non-metallic dish and sprinkle with the salt and the lemon juice. Set aside for 10 minutes.

2 To make the marinade, combine all the ingredients in a small bowl.

3 Thread the cubes of chicken on to pre-soaked wooden skewers. Brush the marinade over the chicken. Cover and set aside to marinate in the refrigerator for at least 2 hours, preferably overnight. Cook the chicken skewers over hot coals, brushing with oil and turning frequently, for 15 minutes, or until cooked through.

4 Meanwhile, combine the yogurt and mint sauce to make the dip and serve with the chicken.

SERVES 4

4 skinless, boneless chicken breasts, cut into 2.5-cm/1-inch cubes
½ tsp salt
4 tbsp lemon or lime juice
vegetable oil, for brushing

marinade
150 ml/5 fl oz low-fat natural yogurt
2 garlic cloves, crushed
2.5-cm/1-inch piece of fresh root ginger, grated
1 tsp ground cumin
1 tsp chilli powder
½ tsp ground coriander
½ tsp ground turmeric

dip
150 ml/5 fl oz low-fat natural yogurt
1 tsp mint sauce

NUTRITION
Calories *173*; Sugars *6 g*; Protein *28 g*; Carbohydrate *6 g*; Fat *4 g*; Saturates *2 g*

 easy

2 hrs 15 mins

8–15 mins

 COOK'S TIP

Try pre-soaking the wooden skewers in water to prevent them from burning when cooking.

This is a colourful dish –
the red of the tomatoes
perfectly complementing
the orange of the
sweet potato.

Thai Red Chicken

SERVES 4

1 tbsp sunflower oil
450 g/1 lb skinless, boneless chicken,
    sliced thinly
2 garlic cloves, crushed
2 tbsp Thai red curry paste
2 tbsp freshly grated galangal or root ginger
1 tbsp tamarind paste
4 lime leaves
600 ml/1 pint coconut milk
225 g/8 oz sweet potato, diced
225 g/8 oz cherry tomatoes, halved
3 tbsp chopped fresh coriander
cooked jasmine or Thai fragrant rice, to serve

1 Heat the sunflower oil in a preheated wok or large, heavy-based frying pan.

2 Add the chicken to the wok and stir-fry for 5 minutes.

3 Add the garlic, curry paste, galangal, tamarind and lime leaves to the wok and stir-fry for about 1 minute.

4 Add the coconut milk and sweet potato to the mixture in the wok and bring to the boil. Allow to bubble over a medium heat for 20 minutes, or until the juices start to thicken and reduce.

5 Add the cherry tomatoes and coriander to the curry and cook for a further 5 minutes, stirring occasionally. Transfer to serving plates and serve hot with jasmine rice.

NUTRITION
Calories *249*; Sugars *14 g*; Protein *26 g*;
Carbohydrate *22 g*; Fat *7 g*; Saturates *2 g*

 easy

15 mins

35 mins

 COOK'S TIP

Galangal is very similar to ginger and is used in Thai cuisine. It can be bought fresh from Oriental food stores, but is also available dried and as a powder. The fresh root needs to be peeled before use.

These chicken wings and corn in a sticky ginger marinade should be eaten with the fingers – there's no other way!

Ginger Chicken *and* Corn

1 Place the corn in a large bowl with the chicken wings.

2 Combine the ginger with the lemon juice, sunflower oil and golden caster sugar in a shallow dish. Mix together until thoroughly combined.

3 Toss the corn and chicken in the ginger mixture to coat evenly.

4 Thread the corn and chicken wings in alternate pieces on to metal or pre-soaked wooden skewers.

5 Cook under a preheated moderate hot grill or on a barbecue for about 15–20 minutes, basting with the ginger glaze and turning frequently until the corn is golden brown and tender and the chicken is cooked. Serve immediately with baked potatoes and salad.

SERVES **4**

3 corn cobs, each cut into 6 pieces
12 chicken wings
2.5-cm/1-inch piece of fresh root ginger, grated or chopped finely
6 tbsp lemon juice
4 tsp sunflower oil
1 tbsp golden caster sugar

to serve
baked potatoes
mixed salad

NUTRITION
Calories *123*; Sugars *3 g*; Protein *14 g*; Carbohydrate *3 g*; Fat *6 g*; Saturates *1 g*

⭐ very easy
🕐 10 mins
🕐 20 mins

 COOK'S TIP

Cut off the wing tips before grilling because they burn very easily. Alternatively, you can cover them with small pieces of foil.

An attractive main course
of chicken breasts filled
with mixed sweet peppers
and set on a delicious
tomato sauce.

Crispy Stuffed Chicken

SERVES 4

4 skinless, boneless chicken breasts, about
   150 g/5½ oz each
4 fresh tarragon sprigs
½ small orange pepper, halved, deseeded
   and sliced
½ small green pepper, halved, deseeded
   and sliced
15 g/½ oz wholemeal breadcrumbs
1 tbsp sesame seeds
4 tbsp lemon juice
1 small red pepper, halved and deseeded
200 g/7 oz canned chopped tomatoes
1 small red chilli, deseeded and chopped
¼ tsp celery salt
salt and pepper
fresh tarragon, to garnish

NUTRITION
Calories *196*; Sugars *4 g*; Protein *29 g*;
Carbohydrate *6 g*; Fat *6 g*; Saturates *2 g*

✪✪✪✪   challenging

   20 mins

   50 mins

1 Make a slit in each of the chicken breasts with a small, sharp knife to create
a pocket. Season inside each pocket with salt and pepper.

2 Place a tarragon sprig and a few slices of orange pepper and green pepper in
each pocket. Place the chicken breasts on a non-stick baking sheet and
sprinkle the breadcrumbs and sesame seeds over them.

3 Spoon 1 tablespoon of the lemon juice over each chicken breast and bake in
a preheated oven, 190°C/375°F/Gas Mark 5, for 35–40 minutes, until the
chicken is tender and cooked through.

4 Meanwhile, preheat the grill to hot. Arrange the red pepper halves, skin side
up, on the rack and cook for 5–6 minutes, until the skin begins to char and
blister. Set the grilled peppers aside to cool for about 10 minutes, then peel
off the skins.

5 Put the red pepper in a blender, add the tomatoes, chilli and celery salt and
process for a few seconds. Season to taste. Alternatively, finely chop the red
pepper and press through a sieve with the tomatoes and chilli.

6 When the chicken is cooked, heat the sauce, spoon a little on to a warm
plate and arrange a chicken breast in the centre. Garnish with tarragon.

This sweet-citrus chicken is delicious hot or cold. Sesame-flavoured noodles are the ideal accompaniment to the hot version.

Sweet *and* Sour Chicken

1 Using a sharp knife, score the chicken breasts with a criss-cross pattern on both sides (making sure that you do not cut all the way through the meat).

2 Combine the honey, soy sauce, lemon rind and juice in a small bowl and season with black pepper.

3 Arrange the chicken breasts on a grill rack and brush with half the honey mixture. Cook under a preheated grill for 10 minutes, then turn over and brush with the remaining mixture. Cook for a further 8–10 minutes, or until cooked through and tender. The juices should run clear when the thickest part of the chicken is pierced with a skewer.

4 Meanwhile, prepare the noodles according to the packet instructions. Drain well and transfer to a warm serving bowl. Add the sesame oil, sesame seeds and lemon rind and toss well to mix. Season with salt and pepper to taste and keep warm.

5 Drain the chicken and serve immediately with a small mound of noodles, garnished with fresh chives and lemon rind.

SERVES 4

4 skinless, boneless chicken breasts, about 125 g/4½ oz each
2 tbsp clear honey
1 tbsp dark soy sauce
1 tsp finely grated lemon rind
1 tbsp lemon juice
salt and pepper

to garnish
1 tbsp chopped fresh chives
grated lemon rind

to serve
225 g/8 oz rice noodles
2 tsp sesame oil
1 tbsp sesame seeds
1 tsp finely grated lemon rind

NUTRITION
Calories *248*; Sugars *8 g*; Protein *30 g*; Carbohydrate *16 g*; Fat *8 g*; Saturates *2 g*

easy

5 mins

25 mins

👨‍🍳 **COOK'S TIP**

These chicken breasts are also ideal for cooking on a barbecue, but ensure the flames have died down and the coals are hot.

Poussins are ideal for a one or two portion meal, and cook very easily and quickly for a special dinner. If you're cooking for one, a microwave makes cooking even quicker and more convenient.

Poussin *with* Dried Fruits

SERVES 4

125 g/4½ oz ready-to-eat dried apples, peaches and prunes
125 ml/4 fl oz boiling water
2 poussins
25 g/1 oz walnut halves
1 tbsp honey
1 tsp ground allspice
1 tbsp walnut oil
salt and pepper

to serve
fresh vegetables
new potatoes

1 Place the fruits in a bowl, cover with the water and leave to stand for about 30 minutes.

2 Cut the poussins in half down the breastbone using a sharp knife, or leave the birds whole.

3 Mix the fruit and any juices with the walnuts, honey and allspice and divide between 2 roasting bags or squares of foil.

4 Brush the poussins with walnut oil and sprinkle with salt and pepper, then place on top of the fruits.

5 Close the roasting bags or fold the foil over to enclose the poussins and bake on a baking sheet in a preheated oven, 190°C/375°F/Gas Mark 5, for 25–30 minutes, or until the juices run clear when the poussins are pierced in the thickest part with a skewer. (To cook in a microwave, use microwave roasting bags and cook on High power for 6–7 minutes each, depending on their size.)

6 Transfer the poussins to a warm plate and serve hot with fresh vegetables and new potatoes.

COOK'S TIP

Cherries, mangoes or paw-paws (papayas) are suitable alternatives to the dried fruit mentioned in this recipe.

NUTRITION
Calories 316; Sugars 23 g; Protein 23 g;
Carbohydrate 23 g; Fat 15 g; Saturates 2 g

          easy

          35 mins

          30 mins

This colourful, nutritious pot-roast could be served for a family meal or special dinner. Add more vegetables if you're feeding a crowd.

Pot-roast Orange Chicken

1 Heat the oil in a large, flameproof casserole and fry the chicken, turning occasionally until evenly browned.

2 Cut one orange in half and place half inside the cavity of the chicken. Place the chicken in the casserole. Arrange the onions and carrots around the chicken. Season with salt and pepper to taste and pour the orange juice over the top.

3 Cut the remaining oranges into thin wedges and tuck around the chicken, among the vegetables.

4 Cover and cook in a preheated oven, 180°C/350°F/Gas Mark 4, for about 1½ hours, or until there is no trace of pink in the juices when the thickest part of the chicken is pierced with a skewer, and the vegetables are tender. Remove the lid and sprinkle with the brandy and sesame seeds. Return to the oven for 10 minutes.

5 To serve, lift the chicken on to a large platter and add the vegetables. Skim any excess fat from the juices. Blend the cornflour with the water, then stir it into the juices and bring to the boil, stirring. Season to taste, then serve the sauce with the chicken.

SERVES 4

2 tbsp sunflower oil
1 chicken, weighing about 1.5 kg/3 lb 5 oz
2 large oranges
2 small onions, quartered
500 g/1 lb 2 oz baby carrots or thin carrots, cut into 5-cm/2-inch lengths
150ml/5 fl oz orange juice
2 tbsp brandy
2 tbsp sesame seeds
1 tbsp cornflour mixed with 1 tbsp water
salt and pepper

NUTRITION
Calories 302; Sugars 17 g; Protein 29 g; Carbohydrate 22 g; Fat 11 g; Saturates 2 g

★★★★ challenging
 10 mins
 2 hrs

5446456565654646466666666666666

LOW FAT

This recipe uses ingredients found in the Languedoc area of France, where cooking over hot embers is a way of life.

Mediterranean Chicken

SERVES 4

4 tbsp low-fat natural yogurt
3 tbsp sun-dried tomato paste
1 tbsp olive oil
15 g/½ oz fresh basil leaves, lightly crushed
2 garlic cloves, chopped roughly
4 chicken quarters
rock salt, to garnish
green salad, to serve

1 Combine the yogurt, tomato paste, olive oil, basil leaves and garlic in a small bowl and stir well to mix.

2 Put the marinade into a dish large enough to hold the chicken quarters in a single layer. Add the chicken quarters. Make sure that the chicken pieces are thoroughly coated in the marinade.

3 Leave to marinate in the refrigerator for 2 hours. Remove and leave covered at room temperature for 30 minutes.

4 Place the chicken over a medium-hot barbecue and cook for 30–40 minutes, turning frequently, until the juices run clear when the thickest part of the chicken is pierced with a skewer.

5 Sprinkle with rock salt and serve hot with a green salad. (It is also delicious eaten cold.)

NUTRITION
Calories *143*; Sugars *4 g*; Protein *13 g*; Carbohydrate *4 g*; Fat *8 g*; Saturates *2 g*

★★ easy
20 mins
50 mins

 COOK'S TIP

For a marinade with an extra zingy flavour combine 2 garlic cloves, coarsely chopped, the juice of 2 lemons and 3 tablespoons of olive oil, and cook in the same way.

With its red and yellow pepper sauces, this quick and simple dish is colourful, healthy and perfect for an impromptu lunch or supper.

Chicken *with* Two Sauces

1 Heat 1 tablespoon of the olive oil in 2 separate medium saucepans. Place half of the chopped onion, 1 of the garlic cloves, the red peppers, cayenne pepper and tomato purée in one pan. Place the remaining onion and garlic, the yellow peppers and basil in the second pan.

2 Cover each pan and cook over a very low heat for 1 hour, until the peppers are very soft. If either mixture becomes dry, add a little water. Transfer the contents of the first pan to a food processor and process, then sieve. Repeat with the contents of the second pan.

3 Return the purées to the separate pans and season with salt and pepper to taste. Gently reheat the sauces while the chicken is cooking.

4 Put the chicken breasts into a frying pan and add the wine and stock. Add the bouquet garni and bring the liquid to the boil. Reduce the heat and simmer over a medium-low heat. Cook the chicken for about 20 minutes, until tender and cooked through.

5 To serve, put a pool of each sauce on to 4 individual serving plates, slice the chicken breasts and arrange them on top. Garnish with fresh herbs and serve immediately.

SERVES 4

2 tbsp olive oil
2 onions, chopped finely
2 garlic cloves, crushed
2 red peppers, halved, deseeded and chopped
pinch of cayenne pepper
2 tsp tomato purée
2 yellow peppers, halved, deseeded and chopped
pinch of dried basil
4 skinless, boneless lean chicken breasts
150 ml/5 fl oz dry white wine
150 ml/5 fl oz Fresh Chicken Stock (see page 14)
Fresh Bouquet Garni (see page 15)
salt and pepper
fresh herbs, to garnish

NUTRITION

Calories 257; Sugars 7 g; Protein 29 g; Carbohydrate 8 g; Fat 10 g; Saturates 2 g

 moderate

10 mins

 1 hr 30 mins

Here, chicken breasts are served with a velvety sauce made from whisky and low-fat crème fraîche.

Chicken *with* Whisky Sauce

SERVES 4

25 g/1 oz butter
55 g/2 oz leeks, shredded
55 g/2 oz carrot, diced
55 g/2 oz celery, diced
4 shallots, sliced
600 ml/1 pint Fresh Chicken Stock
  (see page 14)
6 skinless, boneless chicken breasts
50 ml/2 fl oz whisky
200 ml/7 fl oz low-fat crème fraîche
2 tbsp freshly grated horseradish
1 tsp honey, warmed
1 tsp chopped fresh parsley
salt and pepper
fresh parsley sprigs, to garnish

to serve
vegetable patty
mashed potato
fresh vegetables

NUTRITION
Calories *337*; Sugars *6 g*; Protein *37 g*;
Carbohydrate *6 g*; Fat *15 g*; Saturates *8 g*

easy

5 mins

30 mins

1 Melt the butter in a large saucepan and add the leeks, carrot, celery and shallots and cook for 3 minutes. Add half of the chicken stock and cook for a further 8 minutes.

2 Add the remaining chicken stock, and bring to the boil. Add the chicken breasts and cook for about 10 minutes, or until tender.

3 Remove the chicken with a slotted spoon and cut into thin slices. Place on a large, hot serving dish and keep warm.

4 In another saucepan, heat the whisky until reduced by half. Strain the chicken stock through a fine sieve, add to the whisky is the pan and heat until the liquid is reduced by half.

5 Add the crème fraîche, horseradish and honey. Heat gently and add the fresh parsley and season with salt and pepper to taste.

6 Pour a little of the whisky sauce around the chicken and pour the remaining sauce into a sauceboat to serve.

7 Serve the chicken with a vegetable patty made from the leftover vegetables, mashed potato and fresh vegetables. Garnish with fresh parsley sprigs.

These need to be eaten with your fingers so they are perfect for an informal supper dish.

Sticky Chicken Wings

1 Heat the olive oil in a large, heavy-based frying pan and cook the onion and garlic for about 10 minutes.

2 Add the passata, dried herbs, fennel seeds, red wine vinegar, mustard and cinnamon to the pan along with the sugar, chilli flakes, treacle, and season with salt and pepper to taste. Bring to the boil, then reduce the heat and simmer gently for about 15 minutes, until the sauce has slightly reduced.

3 Put the chicken wings in a large dish, and coat liberally with the sauce. Leave to marinate in the refrigerator for 3 hours, or as long as possible, turning the wings over often in the marinade.

4 Transfer the wings to a clean baking sheet, and roast in a preheated oven, 220°C/425°F/Gas Mark 7, for 10 minutes. Reduce the heat to 190°C/375°F/Gas Mark 5 and cook for 20 minutes, basting often.

5 Serve the chicken wings piping hot, garnished with celery stalks and cherry tomatoes.

SERVES 4

2 tbsp olive oil
1 small onion, chopped finely
2 garlic cloves, crushed
425 ml/15 fl oz passata
2 tsp dried thyme
1 tsp dried oregano
pinch of fennel seeds
3 tbsp red wine vinegar
2 tbsp Dijon mustard
pinch of ground cinnamon
2 tbsp brown sugar
1 tsp dried chilli flakes
2 tbsp black treacle
16 chicken wings
salt and pepper

to garnish
celery stalks
cherry tomatoes

NUTRITION
Calories *165*; Sugars *12 g*; Protein *14 g*;
Carbohydrate *12 g*; Fat *7 g*; Saturates *1 g*

 ★★ easy
 3 hrs 15 mins
🕐 1 hr

👨‍🍳 COOK'S TIP

The longer the chicken is marinated, the more succulent and well-flavoured the dish. If you have time, marinate overnight.

This is perhaps one of the best known Caribbean dishes. The 'jerk' in the name refers to the hot spicy coating.

Jerk Chicken

SERVES 4

4 lean chicken portions
1 bunch spring onions
1–2 Scotch Bonnet chillies, deseeded
1 garlic clove
5-cm/2-inch piece of fresh root ginger, chopped roughly
$\frac{1}{2}$ tsp dried thyme
$\frac{1}{2}$ tsp paprika
$\frac{1}{4}$ tsp ground allspice
pinch of ground cinnamon
pinch of ground cloves
4 tbsp white wine vinegar
3 tbsp light soy sauce
pepper

1 Place the chicken portions in a shallow, non-metallic dish.

2 Place the spring onions, chillies, garlic, ginger, thyme, paprika, allspice, cinnamon, cloves, wine vinegar, soy sauce and pepper to taste in a food processor and process until smooth.

3 Pour the spicy mixture over the chicken. Turn the chicken portions over so that they are well coated in the marinade.

4 Transfer the chicken portions to the refrigerator and leave to marinate for up to 24 hours.

5 Remove the chicken from the marinade and barbecue over medium-hot coals for about 30 minutes, turning the chicken over and basting occasionally with any remaining marinade, until the chicken is browned and cooked through.

6 Transfer the chicken portions to individual serving plates and serve at once.

NUTRITION
Calories 158; Sugars 0.4 g; Protein 29 g;
Carbohydrate 2 g; Fat 4 g; Saturates 1 g

⭐⭐   easy
     24 hrs
    30 mins

The addition of lime juice and lime rind adds a delicious tangy flavour to this chicken stew.

Lime Fricassée *of* Chicken

1 Heat the oil in a large, heavy-based frying pan. Coat the chicken pieces in the seasoned flour and cook for about 4 minutes, until browned all over.

2 Using a slotted spoon, transfer the chicken to a large casserole and sprinkle with the onions.

3 Slowly fry the green and red peppers in the juices in the frying pan.

4 Add the chicken stock, lime juice and rind and cook for a further 5 minutes.

5 Add the chillies, oyster sauce and Worcestershire sauce, mixing well.

6 Season to taste with salt and pepper, then spoon the peppers and juices over the chicken and onions. Cover the casserole with a lid or cooking foil.

7 Cook in the centre of a preheated oven, 190°C/375°F/Gas Mark 5, for 1½ hours, until the chicken is very tender, then serve with lettuce and cress.

SERVES 4

2 tbsp oil
1 large chicken, cut into small portions
55 g/2 oz flour, seasoned
500 g/1 lb 2 oz baby onions or shallots, sliced
1 each green and red pepper, halved, deseeded and sliced thinly
150 ml/5 fl oz Fresh Chicken Stock (see page 14)
rind and juice of 2 limes
2 fresh chillies, chopped
2 tbsp oyster sauce
1 tsp Worcestershire sauce
salt and pepper
lettuce and cress, to serve

NUTRITION
Calories *140*; Sugars *3 g*; Protein *3 g*; Carbohydrate *20 g*; Fat *17 g*; Saturates *1 g*

 moderate
 15 mins
🕐 1 hr 45 mins

👑 COOK'S TIP

Try this casserole with a cheese scone topping: about 30 minutes before the end of cooking time, simply top with rounds of cheese scone dough.

Chilli, tomatoes and corn are typical ingredients in a Mexican dish. This is a quick and easy meal to serve for unexpected guests.

Mexican Chicken

SERVES 4

2 tbsp oil
8 chicken drumsticks
1 onion, chopped finely
1 tsp chilli powder
1 tsp ground coriander
425 g/15 oz canned chopped tomatoes
2 tbsp tomato purée
125 g/4½ oz frozen sweetcorn kernels
salt and pepper

to serve
plain rice
mixed pepper salad

1 Heat the oil in a large, heavy-based frying pan, add the chicken drumsticks and cook over a medium heat until lightly browned on all sides. Remove from the pan and set aside.

2 Add the onion to the pan and cook for 3–4 minutes, until softened, then stir in the chilli powder and ground coriander and cook for a few seconds.

3 Add the chopped tomatoes with their juice and the tomato purée.

4 Return the chicken to the pan and simmer gently for 20 minutes, until the chicken is tender and thoroughly cooked. Add the sweetcorn and cook for a further 3–4 minutes. Season with salt and pepper to taste.

5 Serve with plain rice and mixed pepper salad.

NUTRITION
Calories *207*; Sugars *8 g*; Protein *18 g*;
Carbohydrate *13 g*; Fat *9 g*; Saturates *2 g*

 easy

15 mins

35 mins

 **COOK'S TIP**

If you dislike the heat of the chillies, just leave them out – the chicken will still taste delicious.

These chicken wings are brushed with a simple barbecue glaze, which can be made in minutes, but will be enjoyed by all.

Barbecued Chicken

1 Remove the skin from the chicken if you want to reduce the fat in the dish.

2 To make the barbecue glaze, place the tomato purée, brown fruity sauce, white wine vinegar, honey, oil and garlic in a small bowl. Mix the ingredients together until they are thoroughly blended.

3 Brush the glaze over the chicken. Barbecue over hot coals for 15–20 minutes. Turn the chicken portions over occasionally and baste frequently with the barbecue glaze.

4 If the chicken begins to blacken before it is cooked, raise the rack if possible or move the chicken to a cooler part of the barbecue to slow down the cooking.

5 Transfer the barbecued chicken to warm serving plates and serve with fresh salad leaves.

SERVES 4

8 chicken wings or 1 chicken cut into 8 portions
3 tbsp tomato purée
3 tbsp brown fruity sauce
1 tbsp white wine vinegar
1 tbsp clear honey
1 tbsp olive oil
1 garlic clove, crushed (optional)
salad leaves, to serve

NUTRITION
Calories *143*; Sugars *6 g*; Protein *14 g*; Carbohydrate *6 g*; Fat *7 g*; Saturates *1 g*

⭐⭐ easy

 15 mins

 20 mins

🍳 COOK'S TIP

When poultry is cooked over a very hot barbecue, the heat immediately seals in all of the juices, leaving the meat succulent. For this reason make sure that the coals are hot enough before starting to barbecue.

The stuffing in this recipe is cooked under the breast skin so the flavour is sealed in, and the chicken stays really moist and succulent.

Festive Apple Chicken

SERVES 4

1 chicken, weighing about 2 kg/4 lb 8 oz
oil, to brush
15 g/½ oz butter
2 eating apples, cored and sliced
1 tbsp redcurrant jelly
mixed vegetables, to serve

stuffing

15 g/½ oz butter
1 small onion, chopped finely
55 g/2 oz mushrooms, chopped finely
55 g/2 oz lean smoked ham, chopped finely
25 g/1 oz fresh breadcrumbs
1 tbsp chopped fresh parsley
1 crisp eating apple, cored and grated
  coarsely
1 tbsp lemon juice
salt and pepper

NUTRITION
Calories 219; Sugars 7 g; Protein 29 g;
Carbohydrate 9 g; Fat 8 g; Saturates 4 g

  easy

🕐 10 mins

🕐 2 hrs 15 mins

1 To make the stuffing, melt the butter and fry the onion gently, stirring until softened. Stir in the mushrooms and cook over a moderate heat for 2–3 minutes. Remove from the heat and stir in the ham, breadcrumbs and the fresh parsley.

2 Combine the stuffing mixture with the apple and lemon juice. Season with salt and pepper to taste.

3 Loosen the breast skin of the chicken and carefully spoon the stuffing mixture underneath, smoothing it evenly with your hands.

4 Place the chicken in a roasting tin and brush lightly with oil.

5 Roast the chicken in a preheated oven, 190°C/375°F/Gas Mark 5, for 25 minutes per 500 g/1 lb 2 oz, plus 25 minutes, or until there is no trace of pink in the juices when the chicken is pierced through the thickest part with a skewer. If the breast starts to brown too much, cover the chicken with foil.

6 Melt the butter in a frying pan and sauté the sliced apples in the butter until golden. Stir in the redcurrant jelly and warm through until melted. Serve the chicken with the glazed apples and mixed vegetables.

The richness of the duck meat contrasts well with the apricot sauce. If duckling portions are unavailable, use a whole bird and cut into joints.

Roast Duck *with* Apple

1 Preheat the oven to 190°C/375°F/Gas Mark 5. Place the duck on a wire rack placed over a roasting pan and prick all over with a fork.

2 Brush the duck with the soy sauce. Sprinkle over the sugar and season with pepper. Roast in the oven, basting occasionally, for 50–60 minutes, until the meat is cooked through – the juices should run clear when a skewer is inserted into the thickest part of the meat.

3 Place the apples in a small roasting tin and mix with the lemon juice and honey. Add a few bay leaves and season with salt and pepper to taste. Cook alongside the duck for the last 20–25 minutes of cooking time, basting occasionally, for 20–25 minutes, until tender. Discard the bay leaves.

4 To make the sauce, place the apricots in a blender or food processor together with the juice from the can and the sherry. Process for a few seconds until smooth. Alternatively, mash the apricots with a fork until smooth and mix with the juice and sherry.

5 Just before serving, heat the apricot purée in a small saucepan. Serve the duck with the apple wedges, apricot sauce and fresh vegetables. (Remove the skin from the duck and pat the flesh with kitchen paper to absorb any excess fat, if liked.)

SERVES 4

4 duckling portions, about
    350 g/12 oz each, trimmed
4 tbsp dark soy sauce
2 tbsp light muscovado sugar
2 red-skinned, eating apples, cored and
    cut into wedges
2 green-skinned, eating apples, cored and
    cut into wedges
juice of 1 lemon
2 tbsp clear honey
few bay leaves
salt and pepper
fresh vegetables, to serve

sauce
400 g/14 oz canned apricots, in natural juice
4 tbsp sweet sherry

NUTRITION
Calories *316*; Sugars *38 g*; Protein *25 g*;
Carbohydrate *40 g*; Fat *6 g*; Saturates *1 g*

✪✪✪   moderate

     10 mins

     1 hr 30 mins

The tartness of the citrus fruit goes well with the richness of the duckling. Duck makes a delightful change from chicken for the barbecue.

Citrus Duckling Skewers

SERVES 4

3 skinless, boneless duckling breasts, cut
  into bite-sized pieces
1 small red onion, cut into wedges
1 small aubergine, cut into cubes
lime or lemon wedges, to garnish (optional)

marinade
grated rind and juice of 1 lemon
grated rind and juice of 1 lime
grated rind and juice of 1 orange
1 garlic clove, crushed
1 tsp dried oregano
2 tbsp olive oil
dash of Tabasco sauce

1 Place the duck in a non-metallic bowl with the prepared vegetables.

2 To make the marinade, place all the ingredients in a screw-top jar and shake until well combined. Pour the marinade over the duckling and vegetables and toss to coat. Set aside to marinate in the refrigerator for 30 minutes.

3 Remove the duckling and vegetables from the marinade and thread them in alternate peces on to pre-soaked wooden skewers, reserving the marinade.

4 Barbecue the skewers on an oiled rack over medium hot coals, turning and basting frequently with the reserved marinade, for 15-20 minutes, until the meat is cooked through. Alternatively, cook under a preheated grill.

5 Serve the kebabs, garnished with lime and lemon wedges, if using.

NUTRITION

Calories *205*; Sugars *5 g*; Protein *24 g*;
Carbohydrate *5 g*; Fat *10 g*; Saturates *2 g*

 easy

 45 mins

45 mins

20 mins

🍳 COOK'S TIP

For more zing add 1 teaspoon of chilli sauce to the marinade. The meat can be marinated for several hours, but it is best to marinate the vegetables separately for about 30 minutes.

Prepare these steaks the day before they are needed and serve in toasted ciabatta bread, accompanied by crisp salad leaves.

Glazed Turkey Steaks

1 Place the redcurrant jelly and lime juice in a pan and heat gently until the jelly melts. Add the oil, wine, ginger and nutmeg.

2 Place the turkey steaks in a shallow, non-metallic dish and season with salt and pepper. Pour the marinade over the turkey, turning the meat so that it is well coated. Cover and chill overnight.

3 Remove the turkey, reserving the marinade for basting, and barbecue on an oiled rack over hot coals for about 4 minutes on each side. Baste the turkey steaks frequently with the reserved marinade.

4 Meanwhile, toss the salad leaves in the vinaigrette dressing. Cut the ciabatta loaf in half lengthways and place, cut side down, at the side of the barbecue. Cook the bread until golden. Place each steak on top of a few salad leaves, sandwiched between 2 pieces of bread and serve immediately with cherry tomatoes.

SERVES 4

100 g/3½ oz redcurrant jelly
2 tbsp lime juice
3 tbsp olive oil
2 tbsp dry white wine
¼ tsp ground ginger
pinch of grated nutmeg
4 turkey breast steaks
salt and pepper

to serve
mixed salad leaves
vinaigrette dressing
1 ciabatta loaf
cherry tomatoes

NUTRITION
Calories *219*; Sugars *4 g*; Protein *28 g*;
Carbohydrate *4 g*; Fat *10 g*; Saturates *1 g*

 very easy
 8 hrs 12 mins
 15 mins

🎩 **COOK'S TIP**

Turkey and chicken escalopes are also ideal for cooking on the barbecue. Leave them overnight in a marinade of your choice and cook, basting with a little lemon juice and oil.

Fish *and* Seafood

Naturally low in fat, yet rich in minerals and proteins, white fish and shellfish are ideal to include in a low-fat diet. There are so many different textured and flavoured fish available that they lend themselves to a wide range of cooking methods, as you will see from the recipes that follow. White fish, such as cod, haddock, halibut, monkfish and mullet are readily available and easy to cook. Shellfish such as prawns, oysters, crab and lobster may take a little longer to prepare, but are well worth the effort. Oily fish – like salmon, trout, tuna and mackerel – are high in fat, albeit beneficial oils, and should be eaten in moderation.

These shellfish and vegetable kebabs are ideal for parties. They are quick and easy to prepare and take little time to cook.

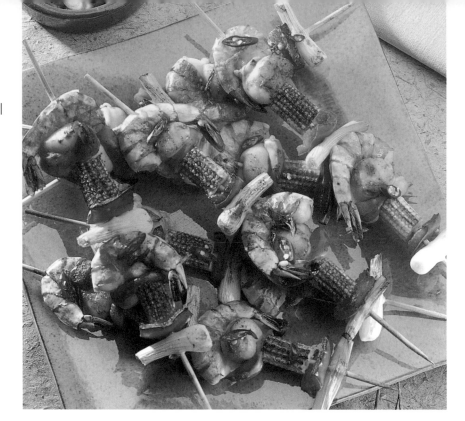

Oriental Shellfish Kebabs

S E R V E S   4

350 g/12 oz raw tiger prawns, peeled leaving tails intact
350 g/12 oz scallops, trimmed and halved (quartered if large)
1 bunch spring onions, sliced into 2.5-cm/1-inch pieces
1 red pepper, halved, deseeded and cubed
100 g/3½ oz baby corn cobs, sliced into 1-cm/½-inch pieces
3 tbsp dark soy sauce
½ tsp hot chilli powder
½ tsp ground ginger
1 tbsp sunflower oil
1 fresh red chilli, deseeded and sliced, to garnish

dip

4 tbsp dark soy sauce
4 tbsp dry sherry
2 tsp clear honey
2.5-cm/1-inch piece of fresh root ginger, grated
1 spring onion, sliced very finely

N U T R I T I O N
Calories *93*; Sugars *1 g*; Protein *15 g*;
Carbohydrate *2 g*; Fat *2 g*; Saturates *0.3 g*

✪✪✪   moderate
🕐   2 hrs 30 mins
🕐   5 mins

1 Divide the prawns, scallops, spring onions, red pepper and baby corn into 12 portions and thread in alternate pieces onto pre-soaked wooden skewers. Cover the ends of the skewers with foil so that they do not burn and place in a shallow dish.

2 Mix together the soy sauce, chilli powder and ground ginger and brush the mixture over the kebabs. Cover and chill for about 2 hours.

3 Preheat the grill to hot. Arrange the kebabs on the rack, brush with oil and cook for 2–3 minutes on each side until the prawns turn pink, the scallops become opaque and the vegetables have softened.

4 Mix together the ingredients for the dip in a bowl.

5 Remove the foil and transfer the kebabs to a warm serving platter. Garnish with sliced chilli and serve with the dip.

Since the scallops are marinated, it is not essential that they are fresh; frozen shellfish are fine for a barbecue.

Scallop Skewers

1 If using wooden skewers, soak 8 skewers in warm water for at least 10 minutes to prevent the food from sticking and the skewers from burning.

2 Combine the lime rind and juice, lemon grass, garlic and chilli together in a pestle and mortar or spice grinder to make a paste.

3 Thread 2 scallops with the corals on to each of the soaked skewers alternating with the lime segments. Cover the ends with foil to prevent them from burning.

4 To make the dressing, whisk together the oil and lemon juice and season with salt and pepper to taste.

5 Coat the scallops with the lime and spice paste and cook for 10 minutes over a medium barbecue, basting occasionally. Turn the skewers once.

6 Toss the rocket, mixed salad leaves and dressing together in a serving bowl.

7 Serve the scallops piping hot, 2 skewers on each plate, with the salad.

SERVES 4

grated rind and juice of 2 limes
2 tbsp chopped finely lemon grass
    or 1 tbsp lemon juice
2 garlic cloves, crushed
1 fresh green chilli, deseeded and chopped
16 scallops, with corals
2 limes, each cut into 8 segments

dressing
2 tbsp sunflower oil
1 tbsp lemon juice
salt and pepper

to serve
55 g/2 oz rocket salad
200 g/7 oz mixed salad leaves

 COOK'S TIP

Ask your fishmonger to prepare the scallops for you, if using fresh ones.

NUTRITION
Calories *182*; Sugars *0 g*; Protein *29 g*;
Carbohydrate *0 g*; Fat *7 g*; Saturates *1 g*

  easy

30 mins

10 mins

The Japanese sauce used here goes particularly well with salmon, although it is usually served with chicken.

Salmon Yakitori

SERVES 4

350 g/12 oz chunky salmon fillet, cut into 5-cm/2-inch chunks
8 baby leeks, cut into 5-cm/2-inch lengths

yakitori sauce
5 tbsp light soy sauce
5 tbsp Fresh Fish Stock (see page 14)
2 tbsp caster sugar
5 tbsp dry white wine
3 tbsp sweet sherry
1 clove garlic, crushed

NUTRITION
Calories *247*; Sugars *10 g*; Protein *19 g*;
Carbohydrate *12 g*; Fat *11 g*; Saturates *2 g*

 easy

 20 mins

15 mins

1 Thread the salmon and leeks alternately on to 8 pre-soaked wooden skewers. Leave to chill in the refrigerator until required.

2 To make the sauce, place all of the ingredients in a small saucepan and heat gently, stirring, until the sugar has dissolved.

3 Bring to the boil, then reduce the heat and simmer for 2 minutes. Strain the sauce through a fine sieve and leave to cool until it is required.

4 Pour about one-third of the sauce into a small dish and set aside to serve with the kebabs.

5 Brush plenty of the remaining sauce over the skewers and cook directly on the barbecue grill rack. (If preferred, place a sheet of oiled kitchen foil on the rack and cook the salmon on that.)

6 Barbecue the salmon and leek kebabs over hot coals for about 10 minutes, or until cooked through, turning once.

7 Baste the kebabs frequently during cooking with the sauce to prevent them drying out. Transfer the kebabs to a large serving platter and serve with a small bowl of the reserved sauce for dipping.

A simple basting sauce is brushed over these tasty kebabs. When served with crusty bread and a green salad, they make a perfect light meal.

Lemony Monkfish Skewers

1 Thread the monkfish, courgettes, lemon, tomatoes and bay leaves alternately on to 4 pre-soaked wooden skewers.

2 To make the basting sauce, combine the oil, lemon juice, thyme, lemon pepper and salt to taste in a small bowl.

3 Brush the basting sauce liberally over the fish kebabs.

4 Barbeque the kebabs for about 15 minutes over medium-hot coals, basting them frequently with the sauce, until the fish has cooked through. Transfer the skewers to plates and serve with green salad leaves and chunks of crusty bread.

SERVES 4

450 g/1 lb monkfish tail, cut into
   5-cm/2-inch chunks
2 courgettes, sliced thickly
1 lemon, cut into wedges
12 cherry tomatoes
8 bay leaves

sauce
3 tbsp olive oil
2 tbsp lemon juice
1 tsp chopped fresh thyme
½ tsp lemon pepper
salt

to serve
green salad leaves
fresh crusty bread

NUTRITION

Calories *191*; Sugars *2 g*; Protein *21 g*;
Carbohydrate *1 g*; Fat *11 g*; Saturates *1 g*

 easy

 10 mins

   15 mins

👨‍🍳 COOK'S TIP

Use plaice fillets instead of the monkfish, if preferred. Allow 2 fillets per person, and skin and cut each one lengthways into 2. Roll up each piece and thread them on to the skewers.

This is a wonderful recipe for a special occasion dish. Cooked with coriander and tomatoes, the scallops have a spicy flavour.

Balti Scallops

SERVES 4

750 g/1 lb 10 oz shelled scallops
2 tbsp oil
2 onions, chopped
3 tomatoes, quartered
2 fresh green chillies, sliced

marinade
3 tbsp chopped fresh coriander
2.5-cm/1-inch piece of fresh root ginger, grated
1 tsp ground coriander
3 tbsp lemon juice
grated rind of 1 lemon
$\frac{1}{4}$ tsp pepper
$\frac{1}{2}$ tsp salt
$\frac{1}{2}$ tsp ground cumin
1 garlic clove, crushed

to garnish
lime wedges
grated orange rind

NUTRITION
Calories *258*; Sugars *2 g*; Protein *44 g*;
Carbohydrate *3 g*; Fat *8 g*; Saturates *1 g*

⭐⭐   easy

🕐   8 hr 15 mins

🕐   15 mins

1 To make the marinade, mix together the ingredients in a bowl.

2 Put the scallops into a bowl. Add the marinade and turn the scallops until they are well coated. Cover and leave to marinate for 1 hour, or overnight in the refrigerator.

3 Heat the oil in a Balti pan or wok, add the onions and stir-fry until softened.

4 Add the tomatoes and chillies and stir-fry for 1 minute.

5 Add the scallops and stir-fry for 6–8 minutes, until the scallops are cooked through, but still succulent inside.

6 Serve garnished with lime wedges and grated orange rind.

 COOK'S TIP

It is best to buy the scallops fresh in the shell with the roe. You will need about 1.5 kg/3 lb 5 oz and ask the fishmonger to clean them and remove the shell for you.

Herbs, onion, green pepper and pumpkin seeds are used to flavour this baked fish dish, which is first marinated in lime juice.

Yucatan Fish

1 Place the cod in a shallow, ovenproof dish and pour the lime juice over. Turn the fish in the juice, season with salt and pepper to taste, cover and refrigerate for 15–30 minutes.

2 Place the green pepper under a preheated moderate grill. Cook, skin-side upwards, until it begins to char and blister. Leave to cool slightly, then peel off the skin and chop the flesh.

3 Heat the oil in a pan and gently fry the onion, garlic, green pepper and pumpkin seeds for 5 minutes, until the onion has softened.

4 Stir in the lime rind, coriander, mixed herbs, mushrooms and seasoning, and spoon the mixture over the fish.

5 Spoon the orange juice over the fish, cover with foil or a lid and place in a preheated oven, 180°C/350°F/Gas Mark 4 for about 30 minutes, or until the fish is just tender.

6 Garnish the fish with lime wedges and fresh mixed herbs, then serve.

SERVES 4

4 cod cutlets, steaks or hake cutlets, about 175 g/6 oz each
2 tbsp lime juice
1 green pepper, halved and deseeded
1 tbsp olive oil
1 onion, chopped finely
1–2 garlic cloves, crushed
40 g/1½ oz green pumpkin seeds
grated rind of ½ lime
1 tbsp chopped fresh coriander or parsley
1 tbsp chopped fresh mixed herbs
55 g/2 oz button mushrooms, sliced thinly
2–3 tbsp fresh orange juice or white wine
salt and pepper

to garnish
lime wedges
fresh mixed herbs

NUTRITION
Calories *248*; Sugars *2 g*; Protein *33 g*; Carbohydrate *3 g*; Fat *11 g*; Saturates *1 g*

✪✪✪ moderate
🕐 30–40 mins
🕐 35 mins

This is a fiery recipe with subtle undertones. Since the flavour of the prawns should still be identifiable, the spices should not dominate this dish.

Prawn Bhuna

SERVES 4

2 dried red chillies, deseeded, if liked
3 fresh green chillies, chopped finely
1 tsp ground turmeric
1/2 tsp pepper
1 tsp paprika
3 garlic cloves, crushed
2 tsp white wine vinegar
1/2 tsp salt
500 g/1 lb 2 oz peeled, raw king prawns
3 tbsp oil
1 onion, chopped very finely
175 ml/6 fl oz water
2 tbsp lemon juice
2 tsp garam masala
fresh coriander sprigs, to garnish

1 Combine the chillies, spices, garlic, vinegar and salt in a non-metallic bowl. Stir in the prawns and set aside for 10 minutes.

2 Heat the oil in a large, heavy-based frying pan or preheated wok, add the onion and cook, stirring occasionally, for 3–4 minutes, until soft.

3 Add the prawns and the spice mixture to the pan and stir-fry over a high heat for 2 minutes. Reduce the heat, add the water and boil for 10 minutes, stirring occasionally, until the water has evaporated.

4 Stir in the lemon juice and garam masala, then transfer the mixture to a warm serving dish and garnish with fresh coriander sprigs.

NUTRITION
Calories *141* Sugars *0.4 g*; Protein *19 g*;
Carbohydrate *1 g*; Fat *7 g*; Saturates *1 g*

 very easy

 15 mins

 20 mins

@ **COOK'S TIP**

Garam masala should be used sparingly and is generally added to foods towards the end of their cooking time. It is also sprinkled over cooked meats, vegetables and pulses as a garnish.

Tuna has a firm flesh, which is ideal for barbecuing, but it can be a little dry unless marinated first.

Charred Tuna Steaks

1 Place the tuna steaks in a single layer in a shallow dish.

2 Combine the light soy sauce, Worcestershire sauce, mustard, sugar and oil in a small bowl. Pour the marinade over the tuna steaks. Gently turn the tuna steaks to coat well.

3 Cover with clingfilm and set aside in the refrigerator to marinate for at least 30 minutes or up to 2 hours.

4 Remove the tuna steaks from the marinade, reserving it for basting. Barbecue over hot coals for 10–15 minutes, turning once and basting frequently with the reserved marinade.

5 Transfer the tuna steaks to warm serving plates. Garnish with flat-leaf parsley and lemon wedges and serve immediately with a green salad.

SERVES 4

4 tuna steaks
3 tbsp light soy sauce
1 tbsp Worcestershire sauce
1 tsp wholegrain mustard
1 tsp caster sugar
1 tbsp sunflower oil
green salad, to serve

to garnish
fresh flat-leaved parsley sprigs
lemon wedges

NUTRITION
Calories *153* Sugars *1 g*; Protein *29 g*;
Carbohydrate *1 g*; Fat *3 g*; Saturates *1 g*

 very easy

 2 hrs 10 mins

 15 mins

🍳 **COOK'S TIP**

If a marinade contains soy sauce, the marinating time should be limited, usually to 2 hours to prevent the fish drying out and becoming tough.

Salmon steaks, poached in a well-flavoured stock and served with a piquant sauce, make a delicious light summer lunch or supper dish.

Poached Salmon

SERVES 4

1 small onion, sliced
1 small carrot, sliced
1 celery stick , sliced
1 bay leaf
rind and juice of ½ orange
a few fresh parsley stalks
salt
5–6 black peppercorns
700 ml/1¼ pints water
4 medium-sized salmon steaks
salad leaves, to serve
lemon twists, to garnish

sauce

1 large avocado, peeled, stoned and chopped roughly
125 ml/4 fl oz low-fat natural yogurt
grated rind and juice of ½ orange
black pepper
a few drops of hot red pepper sauce

NUTRITION
Calories 712; Sugars 5 g; Protein 66 g;
Carbohydrate 6 g; Fat 47 g; Saturates 9 g

 very easy

10 mins

30 mins

1 Put the onion, carrot, celery, bay leaf, orange rind, orange juice, parsley stalks, salt and peppercorns in a saucepan just large enough to take the salmon steaks in a single layer. Pour the water over, cover the saucepan and bring to the boil. Reduce the heat and simmer the stock for 20 minutes.

2 Arrange the salmon steaks in the saucepan, return the stock to the boil. Reduce the heat and simmer for 3 minutes. Cover the saucepan, remove from the heat and leave the salmon to cool in the stock.

3 To make the sauce, place the avocado in a blender or food processor with the yogurt, orange rind and orange juice. Process until smooth, then season with salt, pepper and hot pepper sauce to taste.

4 Using a slotted spoon, remove the salmon steaks from the stock (reserve it to make fish soup or a sauce), skin them and pat dry with kitchen paper.

5 Arrange the salmon steaks on serving plates and spoon a little of the sauce on top of each one and garnish with lemon twists. Serve with the salad leaves and the remaining sauce.

The secret of this dish lies in the simple, fresh flavours which perfectly complement the richness of the barbecued fish.

Mackerel *with* Lime

1 Sprinkle the mackerel with the ground spices and season with salt and pepper to taste. Sprinkle 1 teaspoon of the chopped coriander inside the cavity of each fish.

2 Combine the remaining fresh coriander, chilli, lime rind and juice and the oil in a small bowl. Brush the mixture liberally over the fish.

3 Place the fish in a hinged rack. Barbecue over hot coals for 3–4 minutes on each side, turning the fish once. Brush frequently with the remaining basting mixture.

4 Transfer to individual plates and garnish with chilli flowers, if using, and lime slices, and serve with salad leaves.

SERVES 4

4 small mackerel, gutted and heads removed
¼ tsp ground coriander
¼ tsp ground cumin
4 fresh coriander sprigs
3 tbsp chopped, fresh coriander
1 fresh red chilli, deseeded and chopped
grated rind and juice of 1 lime
2 tbsp sunflower oil
salt and pepper
salad leaves, to serve

to garnish
1 lime, sliced
chilli flowers (optional)

NUTRITION
Calories 302; Sugars 0 g; Protein 21 g;
Carbohydrate 0 g; Fat 24 g; Saturates 4 g

easy

10 mins

10 mins

COOK'S TIP

To make the chilli flowers, cut the tip of 8 small chillies lengthways into thin strips, leaving the chillies intact at the stem end. Remove the seeds and place the chillies in iced water until curled.

The firm, sweet flesh of the trout is enhanced by the spicy flavour of the marinade.

Delicately Spiced Trout

SERVES 4

4 trout, about 175–250 g/ 6–9 oz each, cleaned
3 tbsp oil
1 tsp fennel seeds
1 tsp onion seeds
1 garlic clove, crushed
150 ml/5 fl oz coconut milk or fish stock
3 tbsp tomato purée
55 g/2 oz sultanas
½ tsp garam masala

to garnish
25 g/1 oz cashew nuts, chopped
lemon wedges
fresh coriander sprigs

marinade
4 tbsp lemon juice
2 tbsp chopped fresh coriander
1 tsp ground cumin
½ tsp salt
½ tsp pepper

NUTRITION
Calories 374; Sugars 13 g; Protein 38 g; Carbohydrate 14 g; Fat 19 g; Saturates 3 g

easy
50 mins
20 mins

1 Slash the trout skin in several places on both sides with a sharp knife.

2 To make the marinade, mix all the ingredients together in a bowl.

3 Put the trout in a shallow dish and pour the marinade over. Leave to marinate for 30–40 minutes, turning the fish occasionally.

4 Heat the oil in a preheated wok or Balti pan and fry the fennel seeds and onion seeds until they start popping.

5 Add the garlic, coconut milk and tomato purée and bring the mixture in the wok to the boil.

6 Add the sultanas, garam masala and trout to the wok with the juices from the marinade. Cover and simmer for 5 minutes. Turn the trout over and simmer for a further 10 minutes.

7 Serve garnished with the cashew nuts, lemon and coriander sprigs.

Sea bass is often paired with subtle oriental flavours. Serve the fish with pickled sushi ginger and soy sauce, if liked.

Baked Sea Bass

1 For each fish, lay out a double thickness of foil and oil the top piece well or lay a piece of baking paper over the foil.

2 Place the fish in the middle of the foil and expose the cavities. Divide the spring onion, ginger and garlic between each cavity.

3 Pour the mirin over the fish and season them with salt and pepper to taste.

4 Close the cavities and lay each fish on its side. Fold over the foil to encase the fish and seal the edges securely. Fold each end neatly.

5 Cook over a medium-hot barbecue for 15 minutes, turning once.

6 To serve, remove the foil and cut each fish into 2–3 pieces. Serve with the pickled sushi ginger, if using, accompanied by soy sauce.

SERVES 4

2 sea bass, about 1 kg/2 lb 4 oz each, gutted and scaled
2 spring onions, green part only, cut into strips
5-cm/2-inch piece of fresh root ginger, cut into strips
2 garlic cloves, unpeeled, crushed lightly
2 tbsp mirin or dry sherry
salt and pepper

to serve
pickled sushi ginger (optional)
soy sauce

 COOK'S TIP

Fresh sea bass is just as delicious when cooked very simply. Stuff the fish with garlic and chopped herbs, brush with olive oil and bake in the oven.

NUTRITION
Calories *140*; Sugars *0.1 g*; Protein *29 g*; Carbohydrate *0.1 g*; Fat *1 g*; Saturates *0.2 g*

 easy

10 mins

15 mins

A delicious aromatic coating makes this dish rather special. Serve it with a crisp salad and crusty bread.

Indonesian-style Spicy Cod

SERVES 4

1 lemon grass stalk, outer leaves removed and sliced thinly
1 small red onion, chopped
3 garlic cloves, chopped
2 fresh red chillies, deseeded and chopped
1 tsp grated fresh root ginger
¼ tsp turmeric
2 tbsp butter, cut into small cubes
8 tbsp canned coconut milk
2 tbsp lemon juice
4 cod steaks
salt and pepper
mixed leaf salad, to serve
fresh red chillies, to garnish (optional)

1 Place the lemon grass, onion, garlic, chillies, ginger and turmeric in a food processor and blend until the ingredients are finely chopped. Season with salt and pepper to taste.

2 With the processor running, add the butter, coconut milk and lemon juice and process until well blended.

3 Place the fish in a shallow, non-metallic dish. Pour the coconut mixture over the fish and turn until well coated.

4 Place the cod in a hinged rack, if you have one, which will make them easier to turn. Barbecue over hot coals for 15 minutes, or until the fish is cooked through, turning once. Serve garnished with red chillies, if using, and salad leaves.

NUTRITION
Calories *146*; Sugars *2 g*; Protein *19 g*; Carbohydrate *2 g*; Fat *7 g*; Saturates *4 g*

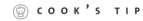 easy
10 mins
15 mins

🍴 **COOK'S TIP**

If you prefer a milder flavour, omit the chillies altogether. For a hotter flavour do not remove the seeds from the chillies.

The marinade for this dish has a distinctly Japanese flavour. Its subtle taste goes particularly well with any type of white fish.

Japanese Plaice

1 Make a few slashes down the sides of each fish so that they absorb the flavours of the marinade.

2 Mix together the soy sauce, sake, sesame oil, lemon juice, sugar, ginger and garlic in a large, shallow dish.

3 Place the fish in the marinade and turn to coat them on both sides. Leave to marinate in the refrigerator for 1 hour.

4 Barbecue the fish over hot coals for about 10 minutes, turning once.

5 Transfer the fish to a serving dish and garnish with the carrot and spring onions. Serve immediately.

SERVES 4

4 small plaice
6 tbsp soy sauce
2 tbsp sake or dry white wine
2 tbsp sesame oil
1 tbsp lemon juice
2 tbsp light muscovado sugar
1 tsp grated fresh root ginger
1 garlic clove, crushed

to garnish
1 small carrot, cut into thin strips
4 spring onions, cut into thin strips

NUTRITION
Calories *207*; Sugars *9 g*; Protein *22 g*; Carbohydrate *10 g*; Fat *8 g*; Saturates *1 g*

 easy

 1 hr 15 mins

1 10 mins

🍴 COOK'S TIP

Use sole instead of the plaice and scatter over some toasted sesame seeds instead of the carrot and spring onions, if preferred.

Here, herrings are filled with an orange-flavoured stuffing and are wrapped in kitchen foil before being baked on the barbecue.

Herrings *with* Tarragon

SERVES 4

4 herrings, gutted and heads removed
salt and pepper
green salad, to serve

stuffing

1 orange
4 spring onions, chopped finely
50 g/1¾ oz fresh wholemeal breadcrumbs
1 tbsp fresh tarragon, chopped

to garnish

1 tbsp light brown sugar
2 oranges, sliced thickly
1 tbsp olive oil
fresh tarragon sprigs

1 To make the stuffing, grate the rind from half of the orange, using a zester. Peel and chop the orange flesh on a plate in order to catch the juices.

2 Mix together the orange flesh, juice, rind, spring onions, breadcrumbs and tarragon in a bowl. Season with salt and pepper to taste.

3 Divide the stuffing into 4 equal portions and use it to fill the body cavities of each fish.

4 Place each fish on to a square of lightly greased kitchen foil and wrap the foil around the fish so that it is completely enclosed. Barbecue over hot coals for 20–30 minutes, until the fish are cooked through – the flesh should be white and firm to the touch.

5 Sprinkle the sugar over the sliced oranges. Just before the fish is cooked, drizzle a little oil over the orange slices and place them on the barbecue for about 5 minutes to heat through.

6 Transfer the fish to serving plates and garnish with the barbecued orange slices and fresh tarragon sprigs. Serve the fish with a fresh green salad.

NUTRITION

Calories *332*; Sugars *4 g*; Protein *21 g*;
Carbohydrate *9 g*; Fat *24 g*; Saturates *6 g*

easy

15 mins

35 mins

Red mullet may be used instead of the snapper, although they are a little more difficult to stuff because of their size. Use one mullet per person.

Steamed Stuffed Snapper

1 Blanch the spinach for 40 seconds, rinse in cold water and drain well, pressing out as much moisture as possible.

2 Arrange the spinach on a heatproof plate and place the fish on top.

3 To make the rice stuffing, combine the cooked rice, ginger, spring onions, soy sauce, sesame oil, star anise and orange in a bowl.

4 Spoon the rice stuffing into the body cavity of the fish, pressing it in well with a spoon.

5 Cover the plate and cook in a steamer for 10 minutes, or until the fish is cooked through.

6 Garnish the fish with orange slices and spring onion and serve.

SERVES 4

175 g/6 oz spinach leaves
1.3 kg/3 lb whole snapper, gutted and scaled

stuffing
55 g/2 oz cooked long grain rice
1 tsp grated fresh root ginger
2 spring onions, chopped finely
2 tsp light soy sauce
1 tsp sesame oil
½ tsp ground star anise
1 orange, segmented and chopped

to garnish
orange slices
spring onion, shredded

NUTRITION
Calories *406*; Sugars *4 g*; Protein *68 g*;
Carbohydrate *9 g*; Fat *9 g*; Saturates *0 g*

 easy

20 mins

 10 mins

COOK'S TIP

The name 'snapper' covers a family of tropical and subtropical fish that vary in colour. They may be red, orange, pink, grey or blue-green. Some are striped or spotted and they range in size from about 15-cm/6-inches to 90-cm/3-ft.

Liven up firm steaks of white fish with a spicy, colourful relish. Use red onions for a slightly sweeter flavour.

Pan-seared Halibut

SERVES 4

1 tsp olive oil
4 halibut steaks, about 175 g/
    6 oz each, skinned
½ tsp cornflour
2 tsp cold water
salt and pepper
2 tbsp snipped fresh chives, to garnish

red onion relish

2 red onions, sliced thinly
6 shallots, sliced thinly
1 tbsp lemon juice
2 tsp olive oil
2 tbsp red wine vinegar
2 tsp caster sugar
150 ml/5 fl oz Fresh Fish Stock (see page 14)

NUTRITION
Calories *197*; Sugars *1 g*; Protein *31 g*;
Carbohydrate *2 g*; Fat *7 g*; Saturates *1 g*

     moderate

30 mins

30 mins

1 To make the relish, place the onions and shallots in a small bowl and toss in the lemon juice.

2 Heat the oil in a heavy-based frying pan and cook the onions and shallots for 3–4 minutes, until just softened.

3 Add the vinegar and sugar and continue to cook for a further 2 minutes over a high heat. Pour in the stock and season with salt and pepper to taste. Bring to the boil, then reduce the heat and simmer gently for a further 8–9 minutes, until the sauce has thickened and slightly reduced.

4 Brush a non-stick, ridged griddle pan with oil and heat until hot. Press the fish steaks into the pan to seal, lower the heat and cook for 4 minutes. Turn the fish over and cook for 4–5 minutes, until cooked through. Drain on kitchen paper and keep warm.

5 Mix the cornflour with the water to make a smooth paste and stir it into the onion relish and heat through, stirring, until thickened. Season to taste.

6 Pile the relish on to 4 warm serving plates and place a halibut steak on top of each. Garnish with fresh chives.

COOK'S TIP
If raw onions make your eyes water, try peeling them under cold, running water. Alternatively, stand back from the onion so that your face isn't directly over it when peeling.

A delicate dish comprising sole fillets rolled up with spinach and prawns, and served in a rich and creamy ginger sauce.

Sole Paupiettes

1 Season the fish fillets and divide the spinach between them, laying the leaves on the skin side. Divide half of the prawns between them. Roll up the fillets from head to tail, enclosing the spinach and prawns, and secure with wooden cocktail sticks. Arrange the rolls on a plate in the base of a bamboo steamer.

2 Stand a low metal trivet in a wok and add enough water to come almost to the top of it, then bring to the boil. Place the bamboo steamer on the trivet, cover with the steamer lid and then the wok lid, or cover tightly with a domed piece of foil. Steam gently for 30 minutes, until the fish is tender and cooked through.

3 Remove the fish rolls and keep warm. Empty the wok and wipe dry with kitchen paper. Heat the oil in the wok, swirling it around until really hot. Add the spring onions and ginger and stir-fry for 1–2 minutes.

4 Add the stock to the wok and bring to the boil. Blend the cornflour with the cream. Add the yogurt and remaining prawns to the wok and heat gently until boiling. Add a little sauce to the blended cream and return it to the wok. Heat gently until thickened and season with salt and pepper to taste.

5 Serve the paupiettes with the sauce spooned over, garnished with whole prawns, if using.

SERVES 4

2 Dover sole, large lemon sole or plaice, filleted
125 g/4½ oz baby spinach leaves
125 g/4½ oz peeled, cooked prawns, thawed if frozen
2 tsp sunflower oil
2–4 spring onions, finely sliced diagonally
2 thin slices of fresh root ginger, chopped finely
150 ml/5 fl oz Fresh Fish Stock (see page 14) or water
2 tsp cornflour
4 tbsp single cream
6 tbsp low-fat natural yogurt
salt and pepper
whole cooked prawns, to garnish (optional)

NUTRITION
Calories 253; Sugars 7 g; Protein 24 g; Carbohydrate 9 g; Fat 14 g; Saturates 5 g

 challenging

 10 mins

45 mins

This flavoursome and colourful fish pie is perfect for a light supper. The addition of smoked salmon gives it a touch of luxury.

Smoky Fish Pie

SERVES 4

900 g/2 lb smoked haddock or cod fillets
600 ml/1 pint skimmed milk
2 bay leaves
115 g/4 oz button mushrooms, quartered
115 g/4 oz frozen peas
115 g/4 oz frozen sweetcorn kernels
675 g/1 lb 8 oz potatoes, diced
5 tbsp low-fat natural yogurt
4 tbsp chopped fresh parsley
55 g/2 oz smoked salmon, sliced into
    thin strips
3 tbsp cornflour
25 g/1 oz smoked cheese, grated
salt and pepper

NUTRITION
Calories *523*; Sugars *15 g*; Protein *58 g*;
Carbohydrate *63 g*; Fat *6 g*; Saturates *2 g*

 challenging
 20 mins
  50–55 mins

1 Place the fish in a pan and add the milk and bay leaves, then bring to the boil. Reduce the heat, cover and simmer for 5 minutes.

2 Add the mushrooms, peas and sweetcorn, return to a simmer, cover and cook for 5–7 minutes. Leave to cool.

3 Place the potatoes in a saucepan, cover with water, bring to the boil and cook for 8 minutes, until tender. Drain well and mash with a fork or a potato masher. Stir in the yogurt, parsley and season with salt and pepper to taste. Set aside.

4 Using a slotted spoon, remove the fish from the pan. Flake the cooked fish, removing the skin and any bones and place in an ovenproof gratin dish. Reserve the cooking liquid.

5 Drain the vegetables, reserving the cooking liquid, and gently stir into the fish with the salmon strips.

6 Blend a little cooking liquid into the cornflour to make a paste. Transfer the rest of the liquid to a saucepan and add the paste. Heat through, stirring, until thickened. Discard the bay leaves and season with salt and pepper to taste. Pour the sauce over the fish and vegetables and mix gently.

7 Spoon the mashed potato over the fish so that is it covered, sprinkle with cheese and bake in a preheated oven, 200°C/400°F/Gas Mark 6, for 25–30 minutes, until golden.

This makes a change from the standard pizza toppings – the base is piled high with seafood and baked with a red pepper and tomato sauce.

Seafood Pizza

1 Place the pizza base mix in a bowl and stir in the dill. Make the dough, according to the packet instructions.

2 Press the dough into a round, about 25-cm/10-inches across, on a baking sheet lined with baking parchment. Set aside to prove.

3 To make the sauce, arrange the red pepper on a grill rack. Cook under a preheated hot grill for 8–10 minutes, until softened and charred. Leave to cool slightly, peel off the skin and chop the flesh.

4 Place the tomatoes and pepper in a saucepan, then bring to the boil. Reduce the heat and simmer for 10 minutes. Stir in the tomato purée and season with salt and pepper to taste.

5 Spread the sauce evenly over the pizza base and top with the seafood. Sprinkle with the capers and olives and top with the cheeses. Bake in a preheated oven, 200°C/400°F/Gas Mark 6, for 25–30 minutes.

6 Garnish with dill sprigs and serve hot.

SERVES 4

140 g/5 oz standard pizza base mix
4 tbsp chopped fresh dill or 2 tbsp dried dill
fresh dill sprigs, to garnish

sauce

1 large red pepper, halved and deseeded
400 g/14 oz canned chopped tomatoes with onion and herbs
3 tbsp tomato purée
salt and pepper

topping

350 g/12 oz assorted cooked seafood, thawed if frozen
1 tbsp capers in brine, drained
25 g/1 oz pitted black olives in brine, drained
25 g/1 oz low-fat Mozzarella cheese, grated
1 tbsp freshly grated Parmesan cheese

NUTRITION
Calories *248*; Sugars *7 g*; Protein *27 g*; Carbohydrate *22 g*; Fat *6 g*; Saturates *1 g*

  challenging

40 mins

45–50 mins

👨‍🍳 **COOK'S TIP**

As an alternative to the pizza base mix, use ready-made pizza bases and brush with a little dill-infused oil.

Vegetables *and* Salads

There is more to the vegetarian diet than lentil roast and nut cutlets. For those of you who have cut out meat and fish completely from your diet, or if you just want to reduce your intake of these ingredients, this chapter offers an exciting assortment of low-fat vegetarian dishes, ranging from pizzas, to curries and bakes. The advantage of vegetable dishes is that very often they are low in fat, and the ingredients can be varied according to personal preference or seasonal availability. Always remember to buy the freshest vegetables available to ensure maximum flavour.

These barbecued tomato cups are filled with a delicious Greek-style combination of herbs, nuts and raisins.

Stuffed Tomatoes

SERVES 4

4 beef tomatoes, halved and deseeded
300 g/10½ oz cooked rice
8 spring onions, chopped
3 tbsp chopped fresh mint
2 tbsp chopped fresh parsley
3 tbsp pine kernels
3 tbsp raisins
2 tsp olive oil
salt and pepper

1 Stand the tomatoes upside down on kitchen paper for a few minutes to allow the juices to drain out, then turn the shells the right way up and sprinkle the insides with salt and pepper.

2 Mix together the rice, spring onions, mint, parsley, pine kernels and raisins.

3 Spoon the rice mixture into the tomato cups.

4 Drizzle a little olive oil over the stuffed tomatoes, then barbecue on an oiled rack over medium-hot coals for about 10 minutes, until they are tender and cooked through.

5 Transfer the barbecued tomatoes to serving plates and serve immediately, while still hot.

NUTRITION

Calories *156*; Sugars *10 g*; Protein *3 g*;
Carbohydrate *22 g*; Fat *7 g*; Saturates *0.7 g*

 easy

10 mins

10 mins

🎩 **COOK'S TIP**

Try grilling slices of beef tomato and onion, brushed with a little oil and topped with sprigs of fresh herbs; or thread cherry tomatoes on to skewers and barbecue for 5–10 minutes.

Soft, creamy rice combines with the flavours of citrus and light aniseed to make this a delicious supper or a substantial starter for six hungry people.

Fragrant Asparagus Risotto

1 Bring a small saucepan of water to the boil and cook the asparagus for 1 minute. Drain and set aside.

2 Pour the stock into a saucepan and bring to the boil, then reduce the heat and maintain a gentle simmer.

3 Carefully melt the low-fat spread with the oil in a large saucepan, taking care that the water in the low-fat spread does not evaporate, and fry the fennel, celery and leeks for 3–4 minutes, until just softened. Add the rice and cook, stirring, for a further 2 minutes, until mixed.

4 Add a ladleful of stock to the pan and cook gently, stirring, until absorbed.

5 Continue adding the stock to the rice, a ladleful at a time, until the rice becomes creamy, thick and tender. This process will take about 25 minutes and should not be hurried.

6 Finely grate the rind and extract the juice from 1 orange and mix into the rice. Carefully remove the peel and pith from the remaining oranges. Holding the fruit over the saucepan, cut out the orange segments and add to the rice, along with any juice.

7 Stir the orange into the rice, along with the asparagus spears. Season with salt and pepper to taste and garnish with the fennel fronds.

SERVES 4

115 g/4 oz fine asparagus spears, trimmed
1.25 litres/2 pints Fresh Vegetable Stock (see page 14)
25 g/1 oz low-fat spread
1 tsp olive oil
2 fennel bulbs, sliced thinly, fronds reserved
2 celery sticks, chopped
2 leeks, shredded
350 g/12 oz arborio rice
3 oranges
salt and pepper

NUTRITION
Calories 223; Sugars 9 g; Protein 6 g; Carbohydrate 40 g; Fat 6 g; Saturates 1 g

★★★　　moderate

🖐　　10 mins

　　35 mins

Ready-made pizza bases
are covered with a chilli-
flavoured tomato sauce
and topped with kidney
beans, cheese and hot
jalapeño chillies.

Mexican-style Pizzas

SERVES 4

4 ready-made individual pizza bases
1 tbsp olive oil
200 g/7 oz canned chopped tomatoes
　with garlic and herbs
2 tbsp tomato purée
200 g/7 oz canned kidney beans, drained
　and rinsed
115 g/4 oz sweetcorn kernels, thawed
　if frozen
1–2 tsp chilli sauce
1 large red onion, shredded
100 g/3½ oz reduced-fat mature Cheddar
　cheese, grated
1 large, fresh green chilli, sliced into rings
salt and pepper

1 Arrange the pizza bases on a baking tray and brush the tops lightly with
　the olive oil.

2 In a bowl, mix together the chopped tomatoes, tomato purée, kidney beans
　and sweetcorn and add chilli sauce to taste. Season with salt and pepper
　to taste.

3 Spread the tomato and kidney bean mixture evenly over each pizza base to
　cover, leaving a narrow rim.

4 Top each pizza with onion and sprinkle with grated cheese and a few slices
　of green chilli to taste.

5 Bake the pizzas in a preheated oven, 220°C/425°F/Gas Mark 7, for about
　20 minutes, or until the vegetables are tender, the cheese has melted and
　the base is crisp and golden.

6 Remove the pizzas from the baking tray and transfer to serving plates.

NUTRITION
Calories *350*; Sugars *8 g*; Protein *18 g*;
Carbohydrate *49 g*; Fat *10 g*; Saturates *3 g*

　easy

　10 mins

　20 mins

🍳 **COOK'S TIP**

Serve a Mexican-style salad with this pizza. Arrange sliced tomatoes, fresh
coriander leaves and a few slices of a small, ripe avocado on a platter. Sprinkle
with fresh lime juice and coarse sea salt.

These Italian pasties are made with pizza dough and are best served hot with salad for a delicious lunch or supper dish.

Potato *and* Tomato Calzone

1 To make the dough, sift the flour into a large mixing bowl and stir in the yeast. Make a well in the centre of the mixture. Stir in the vegetable stock, honey and caraway seeds and bring the mixture together to form a dough.

2 Turn the dough out on to a lightly floured surface and knead for 8 minutes, until smooth. Place the dough in a lightly oiled mixing bowl, cover and leave to rise in a warm place for 1 hour, or until it has doubled in size.

3 Meanwhile, make the filling. Heat the oil in a frying pan and add all the remaining ingredients except for the cheese. Cook for about 5 minutes, stirring occasionally.

4 Divide the risen dough into 4 pieces. On a lightly floured surface, roll each piece into an 18-cm/7-inch circle. Spoon equal amounts of the filling on to one half of each circle. Sprinkle the cheese over the filling. Brush the edge of the dough with milk and fold the dough over to form 4 semi-circles, pressing to seal the edges.

5 Place on a non-stick baking tray and brush with milk. Cook in a preheated oven, 220°C/425°F/Gas Mark 7, for 30 minutes, until golden and risen.

SERVES 4

dough
450 g/1 lb white bread flour
1 tsp easy-blend dried yeast
300 ml/10 fl oz Fresh Vegetable Stock
   (see page 14), warmed
1 tbsp clear honey
1 tsp caraway seeds
skimmed milk, for glazing
vegetable oil, for greasing

filling
1 tbsp vegetable oil
225 g/8 oz waxy potatoes, diced
1 onion, halved and sliced
2 garlic cloves, crushed
40 g/1½ oz sun-dried tomatoes, chopped
2 tbsp chopped fresh basil
2 tbsp tomato purée
2 celery sticks, sliced
50 g/1¾ oz mozzarella cheese, grated

NUTRITION
Calories *524*; Sugars *8 g*; Protein *17 g*;
Carbohydrate *103 g*; Fat *8 g*; Saturates *2 g*

★★★★ challenging
 1 hr 30 mins
 35 mins

This is a variation of the American dish, beef hash, which was made with salt beef and leftovers, and served to sea-faring New Englanders.

Potato Hash

SERVES 4

25 g/1 oz butter
1 red onion, halved and sliced
1 carrot, diced
25 g/1 oz French beans, halved
3 large waxy potatoes, diced
2 tbsp plain flour
600 ml/1 pint Fresh Vegetable Stock (see page 14)
225 g/8 oz tofu, diced
salt and pepper
chopped fresh parsley, to garnish

1 Melt the butter in a frying pan. Add the onion, carrot, French beans and potatoes and fry gently, stirring, for 5–7 minutes, or until the vegetables begin to brown.

2 Add the flour to the frying pan and cook for 1 minute, stirring constantly. Gradually pour in the stock and bring to the boil.

3 Reduce the heat and simmer for 15 minutes, or until the potatoes are tender.

4 Add the tofu to the mixture and cook for a further 5 minutes. Season with salt and pepper to taste.

5 Sprinkle the fresh parsley over the top of the potato hash to garnish, then serve hot from the pan.

NUTRITION
Calories *302*; Sugars *5 g*; Protein *15 g*;
Carbohydrate *40 g*; Fat *10 g*; Saturates *4 g*

 easy

10 mins

 30 mins

🍳 **COOK'S TIP**

Hash is an American term meaning to chop food into small pieces. A traditional hash dish is made from chopped fresh ingredients, such as roast beef or corned beef, peppers, onion and celery, often served with gravy.

An assortment of vegetables is cooked here with tender rice, flavoured and coloured with bright yellow turmeric and other warming Indian spices.

Biryani *with* Onions

1 Place the rice, lentils, bay leaf, spices, onion, cauliflower, carrot, peas and sultanas in a large saucepan. Season with salt and pepper to taste and mix well until combined.

2 Pour in the stock and bring to the boil. Reduce the heat, cover and simmer for 15 minutes, stirring occasionally, until the rice is tender. Remove from the heat and set aside, covered, for 10 minutes to allow the stock to be absorbed. Remove and discard the bay leaf, cardamom pods, cloves and cinnamon stick.

3 To make the caramelized onions, heat the oil in a frying pan. Add the onions and fry them over a medium heat for about 3–4 minutes, until softened. Add the caster sugar, increase the heat and then cook, stirring constantly, for a further 2–3 minutes, until the onions are golden.

4 Gently combine the rice and vegetables and transfer to warm serving plates. Spoon over the caramelized onions and serve immediately with plain, warm naan bread.

SERVES 4

175 g/6 oz basmati rice, rinsed
55 g/2 oz red lentils, rinsed
1 bay leaf
6 cardamom pods, split
1 tsp ground turmeric
6 whole cloves
1 tsp cumin seeds
1 cinnamon stick, broken
1 onion, chopped
225 g/8 oz cauliflower florets
1 large carrot, diced
100 g/3½ oz frozen peas
55 g/2 oz sultanas
600 ml/1 pint Fresh Vegetable Stock (see page 14)
salt and pepper
naan bread, to serve

caramelized onions
2 tsp vegetable oil
1 red onion, shredded
1 onion, shredded
2 tsp caster sugar

NUTRITION
Calories 223; Sugars 18 g; Protein 8 g; Carbohydrate 42 g; Fat 4 g; Saturates 1 g

easy
20 mins
30 mins

Vegetables are cooked in a mildly spiced curry sauce that includes yogurt and fresh coriander.

Creamy Vegetable Curry

SERVES 4

2 tbsp sunflower oil
1 onion, sliced
2 tsp cumin seeds
2 tbsp ground coriander
1 tsp ground turmeric
2 tsp ground ginger
1 tsp chopped fresh red chilli
2 garlic cloves, chopped
400 g/14 oz canned chopped tomatoes
3 tbsp powdered coconut mixed with
    300 ml/10 fl oz boiling water
1 small cauliflower, broken into florets
2 courgettes, sliced
2 carrots, sliced
1 potato, diced
400 g/14 oz canned chickpeas, drained
    and rinsed
150 ml/5 fl oz thick natural yogurt
2 tbsp mango chutney
3 tbsp chopped fresh coriander
salt and pepper
fresh herbs, to garnish
cooked rice, to serve

NUTRITION

Calories *423*; Sugars *24 g*; Protein *16 g*;
Carbohydrate *50 g*; Fat *19 g*; Saturates *7 g*

⭐ very easy
🍳 15 mins
🕐 20 mins

1 Heat the oil in a heavy-based saucepan and fry the onion until softened. Add the cumin seeds, ground coriander, turmeric, ginger, chilli and garlic and fry for 1 minute.

2 Add the tomatoes and coconut mixture and mix well.

3 Add the cauliflower, courgettes, carrots, potato and chickpeas and season with salt and pepper to taste. Cover and simmer for 20 minutes, until the vegetables are tender.

4 Stir in the yogurt, mango chutney and fresh coriander and heat through gently, but do not boil.

5 Transfer to a warm serving dish, garnish with fresh herbs and serve with rice.

 COOK'S TIP

You could use dried chickpeas, soaked overnight, drained and cooked, but canned chickpeas are just as good. Vary the beans, if wished.

This recipe would make a stunning dinner party dish, served with a fresh tomato salad.

Aubergine Pasta Cake

1 Grease and line a 20-cm/8-inch round spring-form cake tin.

2 Place the aubergine slices in a bowl, sprinkle with salt and set aside for 30 minutes to remove any bitter juices. Rinse well under cold running water and drain. Pat dry with kitchen paper.

3 Bring a saucepan of water to the boil and blanch the aubergine slices for 1 minute. Drain and pat dry with kitchen paper. Set aside.

4 Bring another large saucepan of lightly salted water to the boil. Add the pasta shapes, return to the boil and cook for 8–10 minutes, until tender, but still firm to the bite. Drain well and return to the saucepan. Add the soft cheese and allow it to melt over the pasta.

5 Stir in the passata, Parmesan cheese, oregano and salt and pepper.

6 Arrange the aubergine over the base and sides of the tin, overlapping the slices and making sure there are no gaps.

7 Pile the pasta mixture into the tin, packing it down well, and sprinkle with the breadcrumbs. Bake in a preheated oven, 190°C/375°F/Gas Mark 5, for 20 minutes and then leave to stand for 15 minutes.

8 Loosen the cake round the edge with a palette knife and release from the tin. Turn out the pasta cake, aubergine side uppermost, and serve with the tomato salad, garnished with fresh oregano sprigs.

SERVES 4

butter, for greasing
1 aubergine, cut lengthways into 5-mm/½-inch thick slices
300 g/10½ oz tricolour pasta shapes
125 g/4½ oz low-fat soft cheese with garlic and herbs
350ml/12 fl oz passata
70 g/2½ oz Parmesan cheese, freshly grated
1½ tsp dried oregano
25 g/1 oz dry white breadcrumbs
salt and pepper
tomatoes, quartered, to serve
fresh oregano sprigs, to garnish

NUTRITION
Calories *140*; Sugars *4 g*; Protein *14 g*; Carbohydrate *22 g*; Fat *7 g*; Saturates *4 g*

⭐⭐⭐⭐ challenging

🕐 55 mins

🕐 35 mins

These stewed beans form the basis of many Mexican recipes.

Spicy Mexican Beans

SERVES 4

225 g/8 oz dried pinto beans or cannellini beans
1 large onion, sliced
2 garlic cloves, crushed
1 litre /1¾ pints water
salt
chopped fresh coriander or parsley, to garnish

bean stew

2 tbsp oil
1 large onion, sliced
2 garlic cloves, crushed
8 rashers lean streaky bacon, diced
400 g/14 oz canned chopped tomatoes
1 tsp ground cumin
1 tbsp sweet chilli sauce

refried beans

2 tbsp oil
1 onion, chopped
2 garlic cloves, crushed

NUTRITION

Calories 234; Sugars 6 g; Protein 11 g;
Carbohydrate 20 g; Fat 13 g; Saturates 2 g

    easy

    8 hrs

    4 hrs 30 mins

1 Soak the beans in a bowl of cold water overnight. Drain the beans and put them into a saucepan with the onion, garlic and water, then bring to the boil. Reduce the heat, cover and simmer gently for 1½ hours. Stir well, add more boiling water, if necessary, and simmer, covered, for a further 1–1½ hours, or until the beans are tender.

2 When the beans are tender, add salt to taste and continue to cook, uncovered, for about 15 minutes until most of the liquid has evaporated. Serve the basic beans hot sprinkled with fresh coriander. Alternatively, cool, then store in the refrigerator for up to 2 days.

3 To make a bean stew, heat the oil in a heavy-based saucepan and fry the onion, garlic and bacon for 3–4 minutes. Add the remaining ingredients and basic beans and bring to the boil. Reduce the heat, cover and simmer for 30 minutes, then season with salt and pepper to taste.

4 To make refried beans, heat the oil in a heavy-based saucepan and fry the onion and garlic until golden brown. Add a quarter of the basic beans with a little of their liquid and mash. Continue adding and mashing the beans, while simmering gently, until thickened. Adjust the seasoning and serve hot.

COOK'S TIP

Don't add salt until the beans are tender, since it makes them tough.

Roasting the tomatoes gives a sweeter, smoother flavour to the sauce. Italian plum or flavia tomatoes are ideal for this dish.

Basil *and* Tomato Pasta

1 Place the rosemary, garlic and tomatoes, skin-side up, in a shallow roasting tin and drizzle with the oil.

2 Cook under a preheated grill for about 20 minutes, or until the tomato skins have become slightly charred.

3 Peel the skin from the tomatoes. Roughly chop the tomato flesh and place in a saucepan.

4 Squeeze the pulp from the garlic cloves and mix with the tomato flesh and sun-dried tomato paste.

5 Stir the basil into the sauce. Season with salt and pepper to taste.

6 Cook the farfalle in a saucepan of boiling water, according to the packet instructions or until cooked through, but it still has bite. Drain thoroughly.

7 Gently heat the tomato and basil sauce until warmed through.

8 Transfer the farfalle to serving plates and serve with the sauce, garnished with fresh basil leaves.

COOK'S TIP

This sauce tastes just as good served cold in a pasta salad.

SERVES 4

2 fresh rosemary sprigs
2 garlic cloves, unpeeled
450 g/1 lb tomatoes, halved and deseeded
1 tbsp olive oil
1 tbsp sun-dried tomato paste
12 fresh basil leaves, torn into pieces, plus extra to garnish
675 g/1lb 8 oz fresh farfalle or 350 g/12 oz dried
salt and pepper

NUTRITION
Calories 177; Sugars 4 g; Protein 5 g; Carbohydrate 31 g; Fat 4 g; Saturates 1 g

⭐⭐⭐ moderate
 15 mins
 35 mins

The flavours of Mexico are echoed in this dish, in which potato slices are topped with tomatoes and chillies and served with a chunky guacamole.

Mexican Potato Salad

SERVES 4

4 large waxy potatoes, sliced
1 ripe avocado, halved and stoned
1 tsp olive oil
1 tsp lemon juice
1 garlic clove, crushed
1 onion, chopped
2 large tomatoes, sliced
1 fresh green chilli, deseeded and chopped
1 yellow pepper, halved, deseeded and sliced
2 tbsp chopped fresh coriander
salt and pepper
lemon or lime wedges, to garnish

1 Bring a large pan of water to the boil. Add the potato slices, bring back to the boil and cook for 10–15 minutes, until tender. Drain and set aside to cool.

2 Meanwhile, scoop the avocado flesh into a bowl and mash with a fork. (Guacamole is best with a slightly chunky, rather than completely smooth texture.)

3 Add the olive oil, lemon juice, garlic and onion to the avocado flesh and stir to combine. Cover the bowl tightly with clingfilm to minimize discoloration and set aside.

4 Mix the tomatoes, chilli and yellow pepper together and transfer to a salad bowl or serving platter. Add the potato slices and mix gently.

5 Arrange the avocado mixture on top of the salad and sprinkle with the chopped coriander. Season with salt and pepper to taste and serve immediately garnished with lemon wedges.

NUTRITION

Calories *260*; Sugars *6 g*; Protein *6 g*;
Carbohydrate *41 g*; Fat *9 g*; Saturates *2 g*

 easy

20 mins

20 mins

 COOK'S TIP

You can omit the green chilli from this salad if you do not like hot dishes.

This salad is quite deceptive – it is, in fact, surprisingly filling, even though it looks very light.

Grapefruit *and* Coconut Salad

1 Toast the coconut in a dry frying pan over a low heat, stirring constantly, for about 3 minutes, or until it is golden brown. Transfer the toasted coconut to a bowl.

2 Add the light soy sauce, lime juice and water to the toasted coconut and mix together well.

3 Heat the oil in a saucepan and fry the garlic and onion until softened. Stir the onion into the coconut mixture. Remove and discard the garlic.

4 Divide the grapefruit segments between 4 plates. Sprinkle each with the alfalfa sprouts and spoon over the coconut mixture.

SERVES 4

125 g/4¹/₂ oz grated coconut
2 tsp light soy sauce
2 tbsp lime juice
2 tbsp water
2 tsp sunflower oil
1 garlic clove, halved
1 onion, chopped finely
2 large ruby grapefruits, peeled and segmented
90 g/3¹/₄ oz alfalfa sprouts

NUTRITION
Calories *201*; Sugars *133 g*; Protein *3 g*;
Carbohydrate *14 g*; Fat *15 g*; Saturates *9 g*

⭐ very easy
🕙 10 mins
🕙 10 mins

Serve this spicy, Indian-style dish with a low-fat natural yogurt raita for a refreshing contrast.

Hot *and* Spicy Rice Salad

SERVES 4

2 tsp vegetable oil
1 onion, chopped finely
1 fresh red chilli, deseeded and chopped finely
8 cardamom pods
1 tsp ground turmeric
1 tsp garam masala
350 g/12 oz basmati rice, rinsed
700 ml/1¼ pints boiling water
1 orange pepper, halved, deseeded and chopped
225 g/8 oz cauliflower florets, divided into small sprigs
4 ripe tomatoes, peeled, deseeded and chopped
125 g/4½ oz seedless raisins
25 g/1 oz toasted flaked almonds, to garnish
salt and pepper

to serve

raita, made with low-fat yogurt, onion, cucumber and mint

NUTRITION
Calories *329*; Sugars *27 g*; Protein *8 g*; Carbohydrate *59 g*;Fat *8 g*; Saturates *1 g*

  easy

30 mins

35 mins

1 Heat the vegetable oil in a large, heavy-based saucepan. Add the onion, chilli, cardamom pods, turmeric and garam masala to the saucepan and fry over a low heat for 2–3 minutes, until the vegetables have softened.

2 Stir in the rice, boiling water, orange pepper and cauliflower. Season to taste with salt and pepper.

3 Cover the saucepan with a tight-fitting lid and bring the mixture to the boil. Reduce the heat and simmer for 15 minutes, without removing the lid.

4 Uncover the pan and fork through the rice. Stir in the tomatoes and raisins.

5 Cover the saucepan again, turn off the heat and leave for a further 15 minutes. Discard the cardamom pods.

6 Pile the salad on to a warm serving platter and sprinkle with the flaked almonds. Serve the rice salad with a separate bowl of the yogurt raita.

This cooling salad is a good foil for a highly spiced meal. Omit the green chilli, if preferred.

Cool Cucumber Salad

1 Arrange the cucumber slices on a round serving plate.

2 Scatter the chopped chilli, if using, over the cucumber.

3 To make the dressing, mix together the chopped coriander, lemon juice, salt and sugar.

4 Place the cucumber in the refrigerator and leave to chill for at least 1 hour, or until required.

5 When ready to serve, transfer the cucumber to a serving dish. Pour the salad dressing over the cucumber just before serving and garnish with fresh mint and red pepper.

SERVES 4

225 g/8 oz cucumber, sliced thinly
1 fresh green chilli, chopped finely (optional)

to garnish
fresh mint sprigs
red pepper strips

dressing
fresh coriander leaves, chopped finely
2 tbsp lemon juice
½ tsp salt
1 tsp sugar

NUTRITION
Calories 11; Sugars 2 g; Protein 0.4 g;
Carbohydrate 2 g; Fat 0 g; Saturates 0 g

⭐　　　　very easy

🕐　　　　1 hr 15 mins

🕐　　　　0 mins

COOK'S TIP

For the best results you can use a vegetable peeler to thinly slice the cucumber.

Couscous is a type of semolina made from durum wheat. It is wonderful in salads, as it readily absorbs the flavour of the dressing.

Moroccan Salad

SERVES 4

175 g/6 oz couscous
1 bunch spring onions, chopped finely
1 small green pepper, halved, deseeded
    and chopped
10-cm/4-inch piece of cucumber, chopped
175 g/6 oz canned chickpeas, drained
    and rinsed
55 g/2 oz sultanas or raisins
few lettuce leaves
2 oranges, peeled and segmented
salt and pepper
fresh mint sprigs, to garnish

dressing
rind of 1 orange, grated finely
1 tbsp chopped fresh mint
150 ml/5 fl oz natural yogurt

1 Put the couscous into a bowl and cover with boiling water. Leave it to soak for about 15 minutes, until the grains are tender, then stir gently with a fork to separate them.

2 Add the spring onions, green pepper, cucumber, chickpeas and sultanas to the couscous, stirring to combine. Season with salt and pepper to taste.

3 To make the dressing, place the orange rind, mint and yogurt in a bowl and mix together until well combined. Pour the dressing over the couscous mixture and stir to mix well.

4 Arrange the lettuce leaves on 4 serving plates. Divide the couscous mixture between the plates and arrange the orange segments on top. Garnish with fresh mint sprigs and serve.

NUTRITION
Calories *195*; Sugars *15 g*; Protein *8 g*;
Carbohydrate *40 g*; Fat *2 g*; Saturates *0.3 g*

easy

30 mins

0 mins

Home-made coleslaw tastes far superior to any that you can buy. If you make it in advance, add the sunflower seeds just before serving.

Coleslaw

1 To make the dressing, combine the mayonnaise, yogurt, Tabasco sauce and salt and pepper to taste in a small bowl. Leave to chill until required.

2 Combine the cabbage, carrots and green pepper in a large bowl and toss well. Pour the dressing over and toss until the vegetables are coated. Leave to chill until required.

3 Just before serving, place the sunflower seeds on a baking tray and toast them in the oven or under the grill until golden brown.

4 Transfer the salad to a large serving dish, scatter with the sunflower seeds and serve.

SERVES 4

150 ml/5 fl oz low-fat mayonnaise
150 ml/5 fl oz low fat natural yogurt
dash of Tabasco sauce
1 white cabbage, shredded
4 carrots, grated coarsely
1 green pepper, halved, deseeded and
  cut into thin strips
2 tbsp sunflower seeds
salt and pepper

NUTRITION
Calories 224; Sugars 8 g; Protein 3 g;
Carbohydrate 8 g; Fat 20 g; Saturates 3 g

 easy

 10 mins

5 mins

🎩 **COOK'S TIP**

To give the coleslaw a slightly different flavour and texture, try adding one or more of the following ingredients: raisins, grapes, grated apple, chopped walnuts, cubes of cheese or roasted peanuts.

This colourful, summery
salad of crisp vegetables
is tossed in a delicious
sun-dried tomato dressing.

Green Bean *and* Carrot Salad

SERVES 4

350 g/12 oz green beans
225 g/8 oz carrots, cut into thin sticks
1 red onion, sliced thinly
1 red pepper, halved, deseeded and cut
    into thin strips

dressing

2 tbsp extra-virgin olive oil
1 tbsp red wine vinegar
2 tsp sun-dried tomato paste
¼ tsp caster sugar
salt and pepper

1 Blanch the green beans in boiling water for 4 minutes, until just tender. Drain the beans and rinse them under cold water until they are cool. Drain again thoroughly.

2 Transfer the green beans to a large salad bowl. Add the carrots, onion and red pepper to the beans and toss to mix.

3 To make the dressing, place the oil, wine vinegar, sun-dried tomato paste and sugar in a small screw-top jar and season with salt and pepper to taste. Shake vigorously to mix.

4 Pour the dressing over the vegetables and serve immediately or chill in the refrigerator until required.

NUTRITION

Calories *104*; Sugars *9 g*; Protein *2 g*;
Carbohydrate *10 g*; Fat *6 g*; Saturates *1 g*

⭐ very easy

🕐 10 mins

🕐 5 mins

 COOK'S TIP

Use canned beans if fresh ones are unavailable. Rinse off the salty canning liquid and drain well. There is no need to blanch canned beans.

This is a refreshing and very nutritious salad. Add the dressing just before serving to prevent the leaves becoming soggy.

Spinach *and* Orange Salad

1 Slice the top and bottom off each orange with a sharp knife, then remove the peel and pith. Working over a small bowl to collect the juices, carefully slice between the membranes of the orange to remove the segments. Reserve any juices for the salad dressing.

2 Mix together the spinach leaves and orange segments and arrange them in a serving dish. Scatter the onion over the salad.

3 To make the dressing, whisk together the olive oil, orange juice, lemon juice, honey and mustard in a small bowl. Season with salt and pepper to taste.

4 Pour the dressing over the salad just before serving. Toss the salad well to coat the leaves with the dressing.

SERVES 4

2 large oranges
225 g/8 oz baby spinach leaves
½ red onion, chopped

dressing
3 tbsp extra-virgin olive oil
2 tbsp freshly squeezed orange juice
2 tsp lemon juice
1 tsp clear honey
½ tsp wholegrain mustard
salt and pepper

NUTRITION
Calories *126*; Sugars *10 g*; Protein *3 g*; Carbohydrate *10 g*; Fat *9 g*; Saturates *1 g*

⭐ very easy

 10 mins

 0 mins

This is a very refreshing salad. The subtle aniseed flavour of the fennel combines well with the cucumber and mint.

Egg *and* Fennel Salad

SERVES 4

1 fennel bulb, sliced thinly

lemon juice

2 small oranges

1 small cucumber, cut into 12-mm/¹/₂-inch rounds, then quartered

1 tbsp chopped fresh mint

1 tbsp extra-virgin olive oil

2 hard-boiled eggs

1 Place the fennel in a bowl of water with a little lemon juice (see Cook's Tip).

2 Grate the rind of the oranges over a bowl. Using a sharp knife, pare away the orange peel, then segment the orange by carefully slicing between each line of pith. Do this over the bowl to retain any juices.

3 Drain the fennel and mix with the orange segments and juice, cucumber and mint, and mix gently to combine.

4 Pour the olive oil over the fennel and cucumber salad and toss well.

5 Peel and quarter the hard-boiled eggs and use to decorate the top of the salad. Serve at once.

NUTRITION

Calories 90; Sugars 7 g; Protein 4 g; Carbohydrate 7 g; Fat 5 g; Saturates 1 g

 very easy

 25 mins

0 mins

 COOK'S TIP

Fennel discolours if it is left for any length of time without a dressing. To prevent any discoloration, place it in a bowl of water with a little lemon juice.

The sweetness of the pear is a perfect partner to the peppery bite of the radicchio and the piquancy of the cheese.

Pear *and* Roquefort Salad

1 Place the cheese in a bowl and mash with a fork. Gradually blend the yogurt into the cheese to make a smooth dressing. Add the chives and season with pepper to taste.

2 Arrange the salad leaves on a large serving platter or divide them between individual serving plates.

3 Arrange the pear slices over the salad leaves. Drizzle the Roquefort dressing over the pears and garnish with the whole chives.

SERVES 4

55 g/2 oz Roquefort cheese
150 ml/5 fl oz low-fat natural yogurt
2 tbsp snipped fresh chives
few lollo rosso leaves
few radicchio leaves
few lamb's lettuce leaves
2 ripe pears, cored and sliced thinly
pepper
whole fresh chives, to garnish

NUTRITION
Calories *94*; Sugars *10 g*; Protein *5 g*;
Carbohydrate *10 g*; Fat *4 g*; Saturates *3 g*

 very easy

10 mins

 0 mins

🍳 **COOK'S TIP**

Look out for bags of mixed salad leaves as these are generally more economical than buying lots of different types separately.

Desserts

One of the healthiest endings to a meal is fresh fruit topped with low-fat yogurt or fromage frais. Fruit contains no fat and is naturally rich in vitamins and fibre – perfect for the low-fat diet! However, there are many other ways to use fruit as the basis of a range of delicious desserts. Experiment with the unusual and exotic fruits that are increasingly available in our supermarkets. In this chapter there is a mouthwatering range of hot and cold fruit desserts, sophisticated mousses and satisfying cakes, as well as variations on the traditional fruit salad. There is also a number of non-fruit based desserts, such as New Age Spotted Dick and Almond Trifles and even some low-fat treats for chocoholics, such as the super-light Chocolate Cheese Pots and Mocha Swirl Mousse.

A wonderful mixture of summer fruits encased in slices of white bread, which soak up the deep red, flavoursome juices.

Summer Puddings

SERVES 4

butter or vegetable oil, for greasing
6–8 thin slices of white bread,
   crusts removed
175 g/6 oz caster sugar
300 ml/10 fl oz water
225 g/8 oz strawberries
500 g/1 lb 2 oz raspberries
175 g/6 oz blackcurrants and/or redcurrants
175 g/6 oz blackberries or loganberries
fresh mint sprigs, to decorate
pouring cream, to serve

NUTRITION

Calories *174*; Sugars *42 g*; Protein *2 g*;
Carbohydrate *43 g*; Fat *0 g*; Saturates *0 g*

moderate

8 hrs 10 mins

10 mins

1 Grease 6 x 150 ml/5 fl oz moulds with butter. Line the moulds with the bread, cutting it so it fits snugly.

2 Place the sugar in a saucepan with the water and heat gently, stirring frequently, until dissolved, then bring to the boil and boil for 2 minutes.

3 Reserve 6 large strawberries for decoration. Add half of the raspberries and the rest of the fruits to the syrup, cutting the strawberries in half if large. Reduce the heat and simmer gently for a few minutes, until the fruits begin to soften, but still retain their shape.

4 Spoon the fruits and some of the liquid into the prepared moulds. Cover with more slices of bread. Spoon a little juice over the moulds so the bread is well soaked. Cover with a saucer and a heavy weight, leave to cool, then chill thoroughly, preferably overnight.

5 Process the remaining raspberries in a food processor or blender, or press through a non-metallic sieve. Add enough of the liquid from the fruits to give a coating consistency.

6 Turn the puddings out on to serving plates and spoon the raspberry sauce over. Decorate with the mint sprigs and reserved strawberries and serve with cream.

This is like a summer pudding, but it uses fruits that appear later in the year. This dessert requires chilling overnight so prepare in advance.

Autumn Fruit Bread Pudding

1 Place the fruit in a large saucepan with the brown sugar, cinnamon and water, stir and bring to the boil. Reduce the heat and simmer for 5–10 minutes, until the fruits have softened, but still hold their shape.

2 Meanwhile, line the base and sides of a 900 ml/1½ pint pudding basin with the bread slices, ensuring that there are no gaps.

3 Spoon the fruit and some of the juices into the centre of the bread-lined bowl and cover the fruit with the remaining bread. Spoon the rest of the juices over the bread.

4 Place a saucer on top of the pudding and place a heavy weight on top. Chill the pudding in the refrigerator overnight.

5 Turn the pudding out on to a serving plate and serve immediately.

SERVES 4

900 g/2 lb mixed fruit, including blackberries, apples and pears, chopped
150 g/5½ oz soft light brown sugar
1 tsp ground cinnamon
7 tbsp water
225 g/8 oz white bread, sliced thinly, crusts removed (about 12 slices)

NUTRITION
Calories *178*; Sugars *31 g*; Protein *3 g*; Carbohydrate *42 g*; Fat *1 g*; Saturates *0.1 g*

 easy

8 hrs 10 mins

10 mins

 COOK'S TIP

This pudding is delicious served with vanilla ice cream, which counteracts the tartness of the blackberries. Stand the pudding on a plate when chilling to catch any juices that run down the sides of the basin.

An interesting alternative to the familiar and ever-popular summer pudding that uses dried fruits and a tasty malt loaf.

Winter Puddings

SERVES 4

150 g/5½ oz ready-to-eat dried apricots, chopped coarsely
85 g/3 oz dried apple, chopped coarsely
450 ml/16 fl oz orange juice
1 tsp grated orange rind, plus extra to decorate
2 tbsp orange liqueur
325 g/11½ oz fruit malt loaf, cut into 5-mm/¼-inch thick slices
low-fat crème fraîche or low-fat fromage frais, to serve

1 Place the apricots, apple and orange juice in a saucepan, then bring to the boil. Reduce the heat and simmer for 10 minutes. Remove the fruit using a slotted spoon and reserve the liquid. Place the fruit in a dish and set aside to cool. Stir in the orange rind and orange liqueur.

2 Line 4 x 175 ml/6 fl oz pudding basins or ramekin dishes with baking paper.

3 Cut 4 circles from the malt loaf slices to fit the tops of the moulds and cut the remaining slices to line the moulds.

4 Soak the malt loaf slices in the reserved fruit syrup, then arrange around the base and sides of the moulds. Trim away any crusts which overhang the edges. Fill the centres with the chopped fruit, pressing down well, and place the malt loaf circles on top.

5 Cover with baking paper and weigh each basin down with a 225g/8 oz weight or food can. Chill in the refrigerator overnight.

6 Remove the weight and baking paper. Carefully turn the puddings out onto 4 serving plates. Remove the lining paper.

7 Decorate with orange rind and serve the puddings with crème fraîche.

NUTRITION
Calories 447; Sugars 68 g; Protein 9 g; Carbohydrate 80 g; Fat 11 g; Saturates 5 g

 easy

8 hrs 15 mins

15 mins

The sugar lumps give a lovely crunchy topping to this easy blackberry and apple dessert.

Crispy-Topped Fruit Bake

1 Grease and line a 2 lb/900 g loaf pan with a little butter. Place the cooking apples in a pan with the lemon juice, then bring to a boil. Reduce the heat, cover, and simmer for about 10 minutes, until softened and pulpy. Beat well and set aside to cool.

2 Strain the flour, baking powder, and cinnamon into a bowl, adding any husks that remain in the strainer. Stir in ½ cup of the blackberries and the sugar.

3 Make a well in the center of the ingredients and add the egg, yogurt, and cooled apple purée. Mix well to incorporate thoroughly. Spoon the mixture into the prepared loaf pan and smooth the top.

4 Sprinkle with the remaining blackberries, pressing them down into the cake batter, and top with the crushed sugar lumps. Bake in a preheated oven, 375°F/190°C, for 40–45 minutes. Remove from the oven and set aside in the pan to cool.

5 Remove the cake from the pan and peel away the lining paper. Serve dusted with cinnamon and decorated with extra blackberries and apple slices.

SERVES 10

butter or margarine, for greasing
12 oz/350 g tart cooking apples, peeled, cored, and diced
3 tbsp lemon juice
2½ cups self-rising whole-wheat flour
½ tsp baking powder
1 tsp ground cinnamon, plus extra for dusting
¾ cup blackberries, thawed if frozen, plus extra to decorate
¾ cup molasses sugar
1 egg, beaten
scant 1 cup low-fat plain yogurt
2 oz/55 g white or brown sugar lumps, crushed lightly
dessert apple, sliced, to decorate

NUTRITION
Calories 227; Sugars 30 g; Protein 5 g; Carbohydrate 53 g; Fat 1 g; Saturates 0.2 g

⭐⭐⭐   moderate
🕐   15 mins
🕐   55 mins

👨‍🍳 COOK'S TIP

Try replacing the blackberries with blueberries. Use the canned or frozen variety if fresh blueberries are unavailable.

This sweet, fruity loaf is ideal served for tea or as a healthy snack. The fruit spread can be made quickly while the cake is baking in the oven.

Fruit Loaf *with* Apple Spread

SERVES 8

butter or margarine, for greasing
175 g/6 oz rolled oats
100 g/3½ oz light muscovado sugar
1 tsp ground cinnamon
115 g/4 oz sultanas
175 g/6 oz seedless raisins
2 tbsp malt extract
300 ml/10 fl oz unsweetened apple juice
175 g/6 oz self-raising wholemeal flour
1½ tsp baking powder

to serve
strawberries, halved if large
 apple wedges

fruit spread
2 eating apples, cored and chopped
1 tbsp lemon juice
225 g/8 oz strawberries, hulled
300 ml/10 fl oz unsweetened apple juice

1 Grease and line a 900 g/2 lb loaf tin and set aside. Place the oats, sugar, cinnamon, sultanas, raisins and malt extract in a mixing bowl. Pour in the apple juice, stir well and set aside to soak for 30 minutes.

2 Sift in the flour and baking powder, adding any husks that remain in the sieve, and fold in using a metal spoon. Spoon the mixture into the prepared tin and bake in a preheated oven, 180°C/350°F/Gas Mark 4, for 1½ hours, until firm or until a skewer inserted into the centre comes out clean.

3 Remove the tin from the oven and place on a wire rack to cool for about 10 minutes, then turn the loaf out on to the rack and set aside to cool.

4 Meanwhile, make the fruit spread. Toss the apples in the lemon juice, then place in a saucepan with the strawberries. Pour in the apple juice, then bring to the boil. Reduce the heat, cover and simmer for 30 minutes. Beat the sauce well and spoon into a clean, warm jar. Set aside to cool, then seal and label.

5 Serve the loaf with the fruit spread, strawberries and apple wedges.

NUTRITION
Calories 733; Sugars 110 g; Protein 12 g;
Carbohydrate 171 g; Fat 5 g; Saturates 1 g

moderate

1 hr 15 mins

2 hrs

This is a deliciously moist pudding. The sauce is in the centre of the pudding, and oozes out when it is cut.

New Age Spotted Dick

1 Put the raisins in a saucepan with the water. Bring to the boil, then remove from the heat. Leave to sleep for 10 minutes, then drain.

2 Whisk together the oil, sugar and ground almonds until thick and syrupy; this will take about 8 minutes on medium speed, if using an electric whisk.

3 Add the eggs, one at a time, beating well after each addition. Combine the flour and raisins. Stir into the mixture.

4 Brush a 1 litre/1³/4 pint pudding basin with oil, or line with baking paper.

5 Put all the sauce ingredients into a saucepan. Bring to the boil, then reduce the heat, stir and simmer for 10 minutes.

6 Transfer the sponge mixture to the greased basin and pour the hot sauce over the top. Place the bowl on a baking tray.

7 Bake in a preheated oven, 170°C/340°F/Gas Mark 3¹/₂, for about 1 hour. Lay a piece of baking parchment across the top if it starts to brown too fast.

8 Leave to cool for 2–3 minutes before turning it out on to a serving plate.

SERVES 4

125 g/4¹/₂ oz raisins
125 ml/4 fl oz water
125 ml/4 fl oz corn oil, plus a little for brushing
125 g/4¹/₂ oz caster sugar
25 g/1 oz ground almonds
2 eggs, lightly beaten
175 g/6 oz self-raising flour

sauce
55 g/2 oz walnuts, chopped
55 g/2 oz ground almonds
300 ml/10 fl oz semi-skimmed milk
4 tbsp granulated sugar

NUTRITION
Calories 529; Sugars 41 g; Protein 9 g;
Carbohydrate 58 g; Fat 31 g; Saturates 4 g

  easy

  25 mins

🕐 1 hr 15 mins

🍳 **COOK'S TIP**

Always soak raisins before baking them, as they plump up nicely and do not dry out during cooking.

Serve this moist, fruit-laden cake for a special occasion. It would also make an excellent Christmas cake.

Rich Fruit Cake

SERVES 8

butter or margarine, for greasing
175 g/6 oz unsweetened stoned dates, chopped
115 g/4 oz ready-to-eat dried prunes, chopped
200 ml/7 fl oz unsweetened orange juice
2 tbsp treacle
1 tsp finely grated lemon rind
1 tsp finely grated orange rind
225 g/8 oz self-raising wholemeal flour
1 tsp mixed spice
115 g/4 oz seedless raisins
115 g/4 oz golden sultanas
115 g/4 oz currants
115 g/4 oz dried cranberries
3 large eggs, separated

to decorate
1 tbsp apricot jam, warmed
icing sugar, to dust
175 g/6 oz sugarpaste
strips of orange rind
strips of lemon rind

NUTRITION
Calories 772; Sugars 137 g; Protein 14 g; Carbohydrate 179 g; Fat 5 g; Saturates 1 g

 moderate

35 mins

1 hr 45 mins

1 Grease and line a deep 20-cm/8-inch round cake tin. Place the dates and prunes in a saucepan. Pour the orange juice over and simmer for 10 minutes. Remove the saucepan from the heat and beat the fruit mixture until puréed. Add the treacle and lemon and orange rinds. Set aside to cool.

2 Sift the flour and spice into a bowl, adding any husks that remain in the sieve. Add the dried fruits.

3 When the date and prune mixture is cool, whisk in the egg yolks. Spoon the fruit mixture into the dry ingredients and mix together.

4 In a clean bowl, whisk the egg whites until stiff and gently fold into the cake mixture. Transfer to the prepared tin and bake in a preheated oven, 170°C/325°F/ Gas Mark 3, for 1¹/₂ hours. Set aside to cool.

5 Remove the cake from the tin and brush the top with jam. Dust the work surface with icing sugar and roll out the sugarpaste thinly. Lay the sugarpaste over the top of the cake and trim the edges. Decorate with orange and lemon rind.

This melt-in-the-mouth version of a favourite cake has a fraction of the fat of the traditional version.

Carrot *and* Ginger Cake

1 Grease and line a 20-cm/8-inch round cake tin with baking paper.

2 Sift the flour, baking powder, bicarbonate of soda, ground ginger and salt into a bowl. Stir in the sugar, carrots, stem ginger, fresh root ginger and raisins. Beat together the eggs, oil and orange juice, in a separate bowl, then pour into the cake mixture. Mix the ingredients together well.

3 Spoon the mixture into a tin and bake in a preheated oven, 180°C/350°F/ Gas Mark 4, for 1–1¹/₄ hours, until firm to the touch or until a fine skewer inserted into the centre of the cake comes out clean.

4 To make the frosting, place the soft cheese in a bowl and beat to soften. Sift in the icing sugar and add the vanilla essence. Mix well.

5 Remove the cake from the tin and smooth the frosting over the top. Decorate the cake and serve.

SERVES 10

butter, for greasing
225 g/8 oz plain flour
1 tsp baking powder
1 tsp bicarbonate of soda
2 tsp ground ginger
¹/₂ tsp salt
175 g/6 oz light muscovado sugar
225 g/8 oz carrots, grated
2 pieces chopped stem ginger
25 g/1 oz grated fresh root ginger
55 g/2 oz seedless raisins
2 medium eggs, beaten
3 tbsp corn oil
juice of 1 orange

frosting
225 g/8 oz low-fat soft cheese
4 tbsp icing sugar
1 tsp vanilla essence

to decorate
carrot, grated
stem ginger, chopped finely and ground

NUTRITION
Calories *249*; Sugars *28 g*; Protein *7 g*; Carbohydrate *46 g*; Fat *6 g*; Saturates *1 g*

⭐⭐⭐   moderate
🕐   15 mins
🕐   1 hr 15 mins

 COOK'S TIP

You could serve this hot or cold, but the cake improves after a day or two.

A substantial cake that is ideal for tea. The mashed bananas help to keep the cake moist and the lime icing gives it extra zing.

Banana *and* Lime Cake

SERVES 10

butter, for greasing
300 g/10½ oz plain flour
1 tsp salt
1½ tsp baking powder
175 g/6 oz light muscovado sugar
1 tsp grated lime rind
1 egg, beaten
1 banana, mashed with 1 tbsp lime juice
150 ml/5 fl oz low-fat natural fromage frais
115 g/4 oz sultanas

topping
115 g/4 oz icing sugar
1–2 tsp lime juice
½ tsp finely grated lime rind

to decorate
banana chips
finely grated lime rind

1 Grease and line a deep 18-cm/7-inch round cake tin with baking paper.

2 Sift the flour, salt and baking powder into a mixing bowl and stir in the sugar and lime rind.

3 Make a well in the centre of the dry ingredients and add the egg, banana, fromage frais and sultanas. Mix well until thoroughly incorporated.

4 Spoon the mixture into the tin and smooth the surface. Bake in a preheated oven, 180°C/350°F/Gas Mark 4, for 40–45 minutes, until firm to the touch or until a skewer inserted into the centre comes out clean.

5 Leave the cake to cool for 10 minutes, then turn out on to a wire rack.

6 To make the topping, sift the icing sugar into a small bowl and mix with the lime juice to form a soft, but not too runny icing. Stir in the grated lime rind. Drizzle the icing over the cake, letting it run down the sides.

7 Decorate the cake with banana chips and lime rind. Leave the cake to stand for 15 minutes to allow the icing to set.

NUTRITION
Calories *235*; Sugars *31 g*; Protein *5 g*;
Carbohydrate *55 g*; Fat *1 g*; Saturates *0.3 g*

 easy

35 mins

45 mins

Serve this moist, light sponge rolled up with an almond and strawberry fromage frais filling for a delicious tea-time treat.

Strawberry Roulade

1 Line a 35 x 25 cm/14 x 10-inch Swiss roll tin with baking parchment. Put the eggs in a heatproof mixing bowl with the caster sugar. Place the bowl over a saucepan of hot, but not boiling, water and whisk until the mixture is pale and thick.

2 Remove the bowl from the pan. Sieve in the flour and fold into the egg mixture with the hot water. Pour the mixture into the tin and bake in a preheated oven, 220°C/425°F/Gas Mark 7, for about 8–10 minutes, until golden and set.

3 Transfer the sponge to a fresh sheet of baking parchment. Peel off the lining paper and roll up the sponge tightly, using the baking parchment to help it roll. Wrap in a tea towel and set aside to cool.

4 Mix together the fromage frais and the almond essence.

5 Unroll the sponge, spread the fromage frais mixture over the sponge and sprinkle with the sliced strawberries, reserving a few to decorate. Roll the sponge up again and transfer to a serving plate.

6 Sprinkle the strawberry roulade with the flaked almonds and lightly dust with the icing sugar. Decorate with the reserved strawberries to serve.

SERVES 8

3 large eggs
125 g/4½ oz caster sugar
125 g/4½ oz plain flour
1 tbsp hot water

filling
200 ml/7 fl oz low-fat fromage frais
1 tsp almond essence
225 g/8 oz small strawberries, hulled and sliced

to decorate
1 tbsp flaked almonds, toasted
1 tsp icing sugar
a few strawberries

NUTRITION
Calories *166*; Sugars *19 g*; Protein *6 g*;
Carbohydrate *30 g*; Fat *3 g*; Saturates *1 g*

⭐⭐⭐⭐ challenging

 30 mins

 10 mins

The perfect choice for people on a low-fat diet, these little cakes contain no butter, just a little corn oil.

Fruity Muffins

SERVES 10

225 g/8 oz self-raising wholemeal flour
2 tsp baking powder
25 g/1 oz light muscovado sugar
100 g/3¹/₂ oz ready-to-eat dried apricots, chopped finely
1 banana, mashed with 1 tbsp orange juice
1 tsp finely grated orange rind
300 ml/10 fl oz skimmed milk
1 egg, beaten
3 tbsp corn oil
2 tbsp rolled oats
fruit spread, honey or maple syrup, to serve

1 Place 10 paper muffin cases in a deep patty tin. Sift the flour and baking powder into a mixing bowl, adding any husks that remain in the sieve. Stir in the sugar and apricots.

2 Make a well in the centre and add the banana, orange rind, milk, egg and oil. Mix together well to form a thick batter. Divide the batter evenly among the 10 paper cases.

3 Sprinkle with a few rolled oats and bake in a preheated oven, 200°C/400°F/Gas Mark 6, for 25–30 minutes, until well risen and firm to the touch or until a skewer inserted into the centre comes out clean.

4 Transfer the muffins to a wire rack to cool slightly. Serve the muffins while still warm with a little fruit spread.

NUTRITION

Calories *162*; Sugars *11 g*; Protein *4 g*; Carbohydrate *28 g*; Fat *4 g*; Saturates *1 g*

 very easy

 10 mins

10 mins

25–30 mins

COOK'S TIP

If you like dried figs, they make a deliciously crunchy alternative to the apricots; they also go very well with the flavour of orange. Other finely chopped, ready-to-eat dried fruits can be used as well.

This simple, healthy recipe is easy to prepare and cook, but is deliciously satisfying. For a treat, serve hot with low-fat custard.

Baked Pears *with* Cinnamon

1 Brush the pears with the lemon juice to prevent them from discoloring. Place the pears, cored-side down, in a small, non stick roasting tin.

2 Place the sugar, cinnamon and low-fat spread in a small saucepan and heat gently, stirring constantly, until the sugar has dissolved. Keep the heat very low to prevent the water evaporating from the low-fat spread as it gets hot. Spoon the mixture over the pears.

3 Bake the pears in a preheated oven, 200°C/400°F/Gas Mark 6, for 20–25 minutes, or until they are tender and golden, occasionally spooning the sugar mixture over the fruit.

4 To serve, heat the custard in a small saucepan over a low heat, or in a bowl in the microwave, until it is piping hot. Spoon a little over 4 warm dessert plates, then arrange 2 pear halves on each one.

5 Decorate the pears with a little lemon rind and serve immediately.

SERVES 4

4 ripe pears, peeled, cored and halved lengthways
2 tbsp lemon juice
4 tbsp light muscovado sugar
1 tsp ground cinnamon
55 g/2 oz low-fat spread
low-fat custard, to serve
finely shredded lemon rind, to decorate

NUTRITION
Calories *207*; Sugars *35 g*; Protein *3 g*; Carbohydrate *37 g*; Fat *6 g*; Saturates *2 g*

 very easy

 10 mins

 25 mins

COOK'S TIP

For alternative flavours, replace the cinnamon with ground ginger and serve the pears sprinkled with chopped stem ginger in syrup. Alternatively, use ground allspice and spoon over some warmed dark rum to serve.

These bright, fruity little desserts are really easy to make. Serve them with low-fat ice cream and be transported back to childhood!

Apricot *and* Orange Jellies

SERVES 4

125 g/8 oz ready-to-eat dried apricots
300ml/10 fl oz unsweetened orange juice
2 tbsp lemon juice
2–3 tsp clear honey
1 tbsp powdered gelozone
4 tbsp boiling water

to decorate
orange segments
fresh mint sprigs

cinnamon 'cream'
125 g/4½ oz medium-fat ricotta cheese
125 g/4½ oz low-fat plain yogurt
1 tsp ground cinnamon, plus extra to
    decorate
1 tbsp clear honey

1 Place the apricots in a saucepan and pour in the orange juice, then bring to the boil. Reduce the heat, cover and simmer for 15–20 minutes, until the apricots are plump and soft. Leave to cool for 10 minutes.

2 Transfer the mixture to a blender or food processor and blend until smooth. Stir in the lemon juice and add the honey. Pour the mixture into a measuring jug and make up to 600 ml/ 1 pint with cold water.

3 Dissolve the gelozone in the boiling water and then stir it into the apricot mixture in the jug.

4 Pour the mixture into 4 individual moulds, each 150 ml/5 fl oz, or into 1 large mould, 600 ml/1 pint. Leave to chill until set.

5 Meanwhile, make the cinnamon 'cream'. Mix all the ingredients together and place in a small bowl. Cover the mixture and leave to chill until needed.

6 To turn out the jellies, dip the moulds in hot water for a few seconds and invert on to serving plates.

7 Decorate the jellies with the orange segments and sprigs of mint. Serve with the cinnamon 'cream', dusted with a little extra cinnamon.

NUTRITION
Calories *206*; Sugars *36 g*; Protein *8 g*;
Carbohydrate *36 g*; Fat *5 g*; Saturates *3 g*

 easy

4 hrs 15 mins

 25 mins

These tasty morsels are a real treat. Pieces of banana are dipped in caramel and then sprinkled with a few sesame seeds.

Sticky Sesame Bananas

1 Place the bananas in a bowl, spoon over the lemon juice and stir well to coat – this will help prevent them discolouring.

2 Place the sugar and water in a small saucepan and heat gently, stirring constantly, until the sugar dissolves. Bring to the boil and cook for 5–6 minutes, until the mixture caramelizes and turns golden brown.

3 Meanwhile, drain the bananas and blot with kitchen paper to dry. Line a baking sheet or board with baking parchment and arrange the bananas, well spaced apart, on top.

4 When the caramel is ready, drizzle it over the bananas, working quickly because the caramel sets almost instantly. Sprinkle the sesame seeds over the caramelized bananas and set aside to cool for 10 minutes.

5 Mix the fromage frais with the icing sugar and vanilla essence.

6 Peel the bananas away from the baking paper and arrange on serving plates. Serve with the sweetened fromage frais.

SERVES 4

4 ripe medium bananas, cut into
   5-cm/2-inch pieces
3 tbsp lemon juice
115 g/4 oz caster sugar
4 tbsp cold water
2 tbsp sesame seeds
150 ml/5 fl oz low-fat fromage frais
1 tbsp icing sugar
1 tsp vanilla essence

NUTRITION
Calories *215*; Sugars *38 g*; Protein *6 g*;
Carbohydrate *41 g*; Fat *3 g*; Saturates *1 g*

⭐⭐⭐ moderate

  15 mins

🕐 20 mins

These super-light desserts are just the thing if you have a craving for chocolate. Serve them on their own or with a selection of fruits.

Chocolate Cheese Pots

SERVES 4

300 ml/10 fl oz low-fat fromage frais
150 ml/5 fl oz low-fat natural yogurt
2 tbsp icing sugar
4 tsp low-fat drinking chocolate powder
4 tsp cocoa powder
1 tsp vanilla essence
2 tbsp dark rum (optional)
2 egg whites
4 chocolate cake decorations
selection of fresh fruit, to serve

1 Combine the fromage frais and low-fat yogurt in a bowl. Sift in the icing sugar, drinking chocolate and cocoa powder and mix well. Add the vanilla essence and rum, if using.

2 In a clean bowl, whisk the egg whites until stiff. Using a metal spoon, gently fold the egg whites into the chocolate mixture.

3 Spoon the fromage frais and chocolate mixture into 4 small china dessert pots and set aside in the refrigerator to chill for about 30 minutes.

4 Decorate each chocolate cheese pot with a chocolate-cake decoration and serve with an assortment of fresh fruit, such as kiwi fruit, orange, banana, strawberries and raspberries.

NUTRITION

Calories 117; Sugars 17 g; Protein 9 g;
Carbohydrate 18 g; Fat 1 g; Saturates 1 g

 very easy

40 mins

 0 mins

🍳 COOK'S TIP

This mixture would make an excellent filling for a cheesecake. Make the base with crushed amaretti biscuits and egg white, and set the filling with 2 tablespoons gelozone, dissolved in 2 tablespoons of boiling water.

These trifles can be made with any type of fruit, even frozen. When they thaw, the juices will soak into the biscuit base – delicious!

Almond Trifles

1 Divide the amaretti biscuits between 4 serving glasses. Sprinkle over the brandy or liqueur and set aside for about 30 minutes, until softened.

2 Top the biscuits with a layer of raspberries, reserving a few for decoration, and spoon over enough custard just to cover.

3 Combine the fromage frais with the almond essence and spoon the mixture over the custard, smoothing the surface. Chill in the refrigerator for about 30 minutes.

4 Before serving, sprinkle with toasted almonds and dust with cocoa powder.

5 Decorate the trifles with the reserved raspberries and serve immediately.

SERVES 4

8 amaretti biscuits, crushed
4 tbsp brandy or Amaretto liqueur
225 g/8 oz raspberries
300 ml/10 fl oz canned low-fat custard
300 ml/10 fl oz low-fat natural fromage frais
1 tsp almond essence
15 g/½ oz flaked almonds, toasted
1 tsp cocoa powder

NUTRITION
Calories *241*; Sugars *23 g*; Protein *9 g*;
Carbohydrate *35 g*; Fat *6 g*; Saturates *2 g*

 very easy

 1 hr 15 mins

 0 mins

Fruit fools are always popular, and this light, tangy version is no exception. You can use your favourite fruits in this recipe.

Tropical Fruit Fool

SERVES 4

1 ripe mango, stoned and chopped
2 kiwi fruit, chopped
1 banana, chopped
2 tbsp lime juice
½ tsp finely grated lime rind, plus extra
   to decorate
2 egg whites
425 g/15 oz canned low-fat custard
½ tsp vanilla essence
2 passion fruit, halved and seeds scooped
   out (optional)

1 Place the mango in a food processor or blender and process until smooth. Alternatively, mash with a fork.

2 Place the kiwi fruit and banana in a bowl. Toss the fruit in the lime juice and rind and mix well.

3 In a grease-free bowl, whisk the egg whites until stiff and then gently fold in the custard and vanilla essence until thoroughly mixed.

4 In 4 tall glasses, arrange alternate layers of the chopped fruit, mango purée and custard mixture, finishing with the custard on top. Set aside to chill in the refrigerator for 20 minutes.

5 Spoon the passion fruit seeds over the fruit fools. Decorate each serving with the extra lime rind and serve.

NUTRITION
Calories *149*; Sugars *25 g*; Protein *6 g*;
Carbohydrate *32 g*; Fat *0.4 g*; Saturates *0.2 g*

easy

35 mins

0 mins

 **COOK'S TIP**

Other tropical fruits you could try include papaya (paw-paw) purée with chopped pineapple and dates, or pomegranate seeds, to decorate.

A zesty, creamy whip made from yogurt and milk with a hint of orange, and served with light, sweet sponge cakes.

Orange Syllabub

1 Slice off the tops and bottoms of the oranges and the skin, then cut out the segments, removing the zest and membranes between each one. Divide the orange segments between 4 dessert glasses, then chill.

2 In a mixing bowl, combine the yogurt, milk powder, sugar, orange rind and juice, then cover and chill for 1 hour. Whisk the egg whites until stiff, then fold it into the yogurt mixture. Spoon on top of the orange slices and chill for 1 hour.

3 To make the sponge hearts, line a 15 x 25-cm/6 x 10-inch baking tin with baking parchment. Whisk the eggs and caster sugar together until thick and pale. Fold in the sifted flours using a large metal spoon, adding the hot water at the same time.

4 Pour the mixture into the tin and bake in a preheated oven, 220°C/425°F/Gas Mark 7, for 9–10 minutes, until golden and firm to the touch.

5 Turn the sponge out on to a sheet of baking parchment. Using a 5-cm/2-inch heart-shaped cutter, stamp out hearts. Transfer to a wire rack to cool. Lightly dust the hearts with icing sugar.

6 Decorate the syllabubs with grated orange rind and serve with the sponge hearts.

SERVES 4

4 oranges
600 ml/1 pint low-fat natural yogurt
6 tbsp low-fat skimmed milk powder
4 tbsp caster sugar
1 tbsp grated orange rind
4 tbsp orange juice
2 egg whites
grated orange rind, to decorate

sponge hearts
2 eggs
85 g/3 oz caster sugar
40 g/1½ oz plain flour
40 g/1½ oz wholemeal flour
1 tbsp hot water
1 tsp icing sugar

NUTRITION
Calories *464*; Sugars *74 g*; Protein *22 g*; Carbohydrate *8 g*; Fat *5 g*; Saturates *2 g*

⭐⭐⭐ moderate
2 hrs 30 mins
10 mins

Traditionally a rich mixture made with cream, this fruit-based version is just as tempting using low-fat smetana and fromage frais as a topping.

Mixed Fruit Brûlées

SERVES 4

450 g/1 lb prepared assorted summer fruits, such as strawberries, raspberries, blackcurrants, redcurrants and cherries, thawed if frozen
150 ml/5 fl oz smetana (buttermilk)
150 ml/5 fl oz low-fat natural fromage frais
1 tsp vanilla essence
4 tbsp demerara sugar

1 Divide the prepared strawberries, raspberries, blackcurrants, redcurrants and cherries evenly among 4 small heatproof ramekin dishes.

2 Combine the smetana, fromage frais and vanilla essence. Spoon the mixture over the fruit, to cover it completely.

3 Top each serving with 1 tablespoon demerara sugar and place the desserts under a preheated grill for 2–3 minutes, until the sugar melts completely and begins to caramelise. Set the mixed fruit brûlées aside for a couple of minutes before serving.

NUTRITION

Calories *165*; Sugars *21 g*; Protein *5 g*; Carbohydrate *21 g*; Fat *7 g*; Saturates *5 g*

very easy

5 mins

5 mins

🍳 COOK'S TIP

Vegetarians should read the labels carefully when buying low-fat products, such as fromage frais, as some brands are thickened with non-vegetarian gelatine and other additives.

This fruit meringue dish was created for Anna Pavlova, and it looks very impressive. Use fruits of your choice to make a colourful display.

Pavlova

1 Line a baking sheet with baking parchment and mark out a 30-cm/12-inch diameter circle.

2 Whisk the egg whites and cream of tartar together until stiff. Gradually beat in the caster sugar and vanilla essence. Whisk well until glossy and stiff.

3 Spoon or pipe the meringue mixture into the marked circle, in an even layer, slightly raised at the edges to form a dip in the centre.

4 Baking the meringue depends on your preference. If you like a soft chewy meringue, bake at 140°C/275°F/ Gas Mark 1 for about 1¹/₂ hours, until cooked, but slightly soft in the centre. If you prefer a drier meringue, bake in the oven at 110°C/225°F/Gas Mark ¹/₄, for 3 hours, until cooked.

5 Before serving, whip the cream to a piping consistency, and either spoon or pipe on to the meringue base, leaving a border around the edge.

6 Stir the strawberries and liqueur together and spoon on to the cream. Decorate with fruits of your choice.

SERVES 4

6 egg whites
¹/₂ tsp cream of tartar
225 g/8 oz caster sugar
1 tsp vanilla flavouring
300 ml/10 fl oz whipping cream
400 g/14 oz strawberries, hulled and halved
3 tbsp orange-flavoured liqueur
fruits of your choice, to decorate

 COOK'S TIP

If you like a dry meringue, you can leave it in the oven on the lowest setting overnight. However, do not use this technique with a gas oven – in an electric oven or solid fuel cooker it is fine.

NUTRITION
Calories *321*; Sugars *37 g*; Protein *3 g*;
Carbohydrate *37 g*; Fat *18 g*; Saturates *11 g*

⭐⭐⭐   moderate

🕐   30 mins

🕐   1 hr 30 mins–3 hrs

These creamy cheese desserts are so delicious that it's hard to believe that they are low in fat.

Almond Cheesecakes

SERVES 4

12 amaretti biscuits, crushed
1 egg white, beaten lightly
225 g/8 oz skimmed-milk soft cheese
½ tsp almond essence
½ tsp finely grated lime rind
25 g/1 oz ground almonds
25 g/1 oz caster sugar
55 g/2 oz sultanas
2 tsp powdered gelozone
2 tbsp boiling water
2 tbsp lime juice

to decorate
25 g/1 oz flaked toasted almonds
lime rind, cut into strips

1 Place the amaretti biscuits in a bowl and bind together with the egg white.

2 Arrange 4 non-stick pastry rings or poached egg rings, 9-cm/3½-inches across, on a baking tray lined with baking paper. Divide the biscuit mixture between the rings, pressing down well. Bake in a preheated oven, 180°C/350°F/Gas Mark 4, for 10 minutes, until crisp. Remove from the oven and leave to cool in the rings.

3 Beat the soft cheese, then beat in the almond essence, lime rind, ground almonds, sugar and sultanas until thoroughly combined.

4 Dissolve the gelozone in the boiling water and stir in the lime juice. Fold into the cheese mixture and spoon over the biscuit bases. Smooth over the tops and chill for 1 hour, or until set.

5 Loosen the cheesecakes from the tins using a small palette knife or spatula and transfer to serving plates. Decorate with flaked toasted almonds and lime rind, and serve.

NUTRITION
Calories *361*; Sugars *29 g*; Protein *16 g*;
Carbohydrate *43 g*; Fat *15 g*; Saturates *4 g*

easy

 1 hr 15 mins

 10 mins

A combination of feather-light yet richly moreish, these chocolate and coffee mousses are attractively presented in tall glasses.

Mocha Swirl Mousse

1 Place the coffee and chicory essence in a bowl, and the cocoa powder and drinking chocolate in a second bowl. Divide the crème fraîche between the 2 bowls and mix both well.

2 Dissolve the gelozone in the boiling water and set aside. In a grease-free bowl, whisk the egg whites and sugar until stiff and divide this evenly between the two mixtures.

3 Divide the dissolved gelozone between the 2 mixtures and, using a large metal spoon, gently fold, until well mixed.

4 Spoon small amounts of the 2 mousses alternately into 4 serving glasses and swirl together gently. Place in the refrigerator and chill for about 1 hour, or until set.

5 To serve, top each mousse with a teaspoonful of crème fraîche, a chocolate coffee bean and a light dusting of cocoa powder. Serve immediately.

SERVES 4

1 tbsp coffee and chicory essence
2 tsp cocoa powder, plus extra for dusting
1 tsp low-fat drinking chocolate powder
150 ml/5 fl oz low-fat crème fraîche, plus 4 tsp to serve
2 tsp powdered gelozone
2 tbsp boiling water
2 large egg whites
2 tbsp caster sugar
4 chocolate coffee beans, to serve

NUTRITION
Calories 136; Sugars 10 g; Protein 5 g; Carbohydrate 11 g; Fat 8 g; Saturates 5 g

 easy

 1 hr 15 mins

 0 mins

COOK'S TIP

Gelozone, the vegetarian equivalent of gelatine, is available from most health food shops.

Index